Channel

Guide to

FORM and BETTING

CHANNEL FOUR RACING GUIDES

edited by Sean Magee

also available

RACEHORSES
with John Francome

RACECOURSES
with Derek Thompson

The Channel Four Racing Guide to FORM and BETTING

NEW UPDATED EDITION

with

JIM McGRATH and JOHN McCRIRICK

and members of the Channel Four Racing team

edited by

SEAN MAGEE

First published in 1998 by Channel 4 Books
This edition published in 2001 by Channel 4 Books,
an imprint of Macmillan Publishers Ltd,
25 Eccleston Place London SW1W 9NF, Basingstoke and Oxford

www.macmillan.com

Associated companies throughout the world

ISBN 07522 1970 7

1 3 5 7 9 8 6 4 2

A CIP catalogue record for this book is available from the British Library.

Design by Production Line
Printed and bound by Mackays of Chatham, plc, Chatham, Kent

This book accompanies the television series Channel 4 Racing
made by Highflyer Productions for Channel 4.
Executive Producers: John Fairley and Andrew Franklin

Contents

Acknowledgements

The racecard for the Pillar Property Chase at Cheltenham on page 57 is reproduced by kind permission of the *Racing Post*, as are the other illustrations from that paper on page 63. The official form-book record of that race is reproduced by kind permission of Raceform Ltd.

Words of wisdom from the Channel Four Racing team

Jim McGrath and John McCririck provide detailed guidance in the main part of this book. But what nuggets of advice do the other members of the team offer?

Mike Cattermole

'If you are at the course, always try and make time to visit the parade ring before placing your bet. I have changed my mind about a race on many occasions after looking at the runners in close-up. Occasionally you can be deceived but you can save a lot of losing bets this way and you may even pick out an unlikely winner simply from the way a horse looks.

'Also, limit your stake to what you can afford. If you are going to miss your tenner, then don't bet. If, on the other hand, you know that missing a few hundred quid in losing bets won't make a blind bit of difference to your outlook on life, then lucky old you!'

Alastair Down

'I have two rules in betting, although my bank manager wishes it were more.

'First, never bet odds on, and secondly – and this should be branded on every racegoer's forehead – always check the Tote.

'If you were faced with two bookmakers' boards, with one offering 12–1 and the other 22–1, would you take the twelves? Yet by ignoring the Tote, punters often do just that, and those who persist in the habit deserve sectioning under the 1959 Mental Health Act.

'At big meetings especially, the Tote can offer tremendous value, particularly for horses from small yards or ridden by jockeys not in the first flush of fashion. So always check the old nanny goat – you're betting against your fellow punters, rather than the bookies, and sometimes the benefits can prove wallet-stuffingly spectacular.'

John Francome

'Watch horses, and follow the ones that really catch your eye: you can often do well by spotting a few improving three-year-olds and sticking with those. Always remember: you don't have to bet – so if you don't have a sound reason for betting, leave that race alone.'

Graham Goode

'Work out what you think the price of your selection should be, and only bet if the odds are better. Make betting a business by keeping a true record of selections, then you can work out the profit on turnover. If you fritter for fun you'll fail in the long run.'

Lesley Graham

'As the smallest of small-time punters – and certainly the smallest in the Channel Four Racing team! – I wouldn't pretend to have any great betting secret. But there's one piece of advice that every punter, big or small, must stick to religiously – never chase your losses.'

Simon Holt

'Having faith in your own judgement is possibly the best advice I can give, particularly if you have been following horse racing for long enough to form an opinion and know when you have seen a good horse or witnessed a promising performance. Follow those instincts and you may be pleasantly surprised how often you are right.'

John Oaksey

'Back in my riding days I was knocked out by a fall at Folkestone, and on my discharge from hospital – still suffering from the bang to the head – I staked hugely more than my usual bet in a £25 each-way Yankee: total stake £550. Three of the four came in, and had L. Piggott woken his ideas up on John Cherry in the Chester Cup I would have won over £20,000. As it was, I collected about £3,000, so I wasn't complaining too bitterly. Moral: bet only when suffering the effects of concussion.'

Brough Scott

'Avoid stables that are out of form, and follow stables in form. Follow apprentices in form when they get hot.'

Derek Thompson

'Never bet odds on – it's as simple as that!'

Walter Swinburn

'Having been a jockey for twenty-odd years I am no expert on gambling. However what I have learned is not to go looking for a reason to bet, but to wait for something that stands out and excites you, and then to trust your own judgement.'

Top of the form

Jim McGrath

Solid study of the form book is essential for anyone who wants to take their betting seriously.

Just consider. The majority of races are won by the first or second favourites. In many races their positions in the betting market have been earned by their previous performances – i.e. through their 'form'. Therefore, the outcome of many races is predictable through careful form study, and the more time you can devote to that, the better you'll bet.

There are virtually no short cuts, and to arrive properly at your decisions you must be prepared to sift through all the facts.

During the Flat season there are so many meetings that no one is able to give due attention to every race. So, when your time is limited, it generally pays to concentrate on the better races, such events usually attracting good horses prepared by leading trainers and ridden by top jockeys. The form of these is more likely to prove reliable than those at a lower level.

Form study is a vital element in picking winners, but not the only one. If possible it needs to be combined with having a good look at the horses before a race – either on television or, ideally, in the flesh at the racecourse. Learn the characteristics of individual horses, and assess their chances accordingly. For example, when on song that fine stayer Celeric would invariably buck and kick in the paddock. But, when he looked half asleep in the parade ring, he usually didn't run anything like so well.

As for the 'iron horse' of the 2000 Flat season, Giant's Causeway. Well, he often got a shade warm and behaved mulishly at the stalls. However, neither trait adversely affected his performances. Nonetheless, the same behaviour from another horse could well signal a nervousness which might affect his running.

Get to know horses, and take any facts you can glean about them alongside the study you have made of their form.

The overriding moral: *don't take form at face value.*

• • •

However much time you have to devote to studying form, and however seriously you take your betting, there are a few basics well worth marking on the first page of your form book:

Know your horses

Watch horses closely, in particular the better ones, and not just when they're in action – knowing how they react before a race can be a definite help in predicting how they might perform in it. John Francome has a great eye for a horse and has proved time after time that studying the runners in the paddock really does pay. Remember Moonax, his paddock 'eyecatcher' on Channel Four before the 1994 St Leger? The Barry Hills-trained colt didn't appear to have the form to win but, to John, stood out on looks – and obliged at 40–1. Franks will never, ever, back a horse that doesn't look well.

By studying how past races were run, you can build up a picture of individual horses' racing styles. Are they front-runners or better suited to being held up? Such knowledge will help you to anticipate how the race you are currently studying will unfold, a vital asset in forming your final decision.

Why? Because every horse's style of running is a crucial aspect of its form profile. Say there are several front-runners in a race: they might well cut each other's throats, allowing one who needs to be held up to come through late. Equally, if there is no obvious pacemaker, is there a horse who might benefit from enterprising jockeyship? Some horses, reliable as they may be, simply feel they have done enough once hitting the front and start to doss. Therefore it would do nothing for their chances if they were forced to make the pace. Others are more versatile.

The moral once again is: *get to know your horses.*

The going factor

When Phil Bull, founder of Timeform and perhaps the greatest betting brain of the last century, was interviewing prospective recruits for positions in that company, one of the questions he always posed was: What is the most important fact a punter needs to know before having a bet on a horse? The answer? The state of the ground.

Horses, like humans, are built in different ways, and their action – their manner of running – also differs. For simple physical reasons, few are able to turn in the same level of performance on firm and heavy ground. As a horse's racing record builds up, astute punters construct a picture of which going suits it ideally.

But it also pays to appreciate the difference between the same status of going at different courses, as this can influence how you assess a performance. Chepstow, for example, often becomes especially heavy when conditions are very wet, as does Aintree. The last few years have seen runnings of the Grand National in ground so heavy that only a few horses have managed to complete: just six in 1994, Miinnehoma's year, and six again in 1998 when Earth Summit and Suny Bay drew well clear in desperate conditions. Lingfield Park is another course where conditions become very testing in heavy ground.

When weighing up form in such circumstances, punters must take into account that fields will almost invariably return strung out – and that the distances separating the runners at the finish don't truly reflect their relative merits.

On the other hand, there is rarely genuinely soft going at Newmarket, a course which drains well, and Doncaster doesn't often get seriously testing for Flat racing. A little course knowledge can definitely be of some help.

Incidentally, with modern watering systems providing a much more sophisticated form of irrigation than was available fifteen or so years ago, it is rarely the case that one side of a track will be genuinely faster than another, so take warily any pronouncements to that effect. There are exceptions. The camber in the straight at Epsom Downs means that in very wet conditions the ground is usually worse on the inside (the lower) part of the track, and, when they obtain, jockeys often tack across to the stands side.

Whatever the horse, whatever the course, whatever the race: always take account of the ground, and never forget that horses unable to act effectively on the prevailing going are most unlikely to run to form.

Horses for courses

The idea of horses for courses is based on the very simple notion that a horse who has won on a particular course is suited by its conformation and therefore can be expected to go well on it again. But, as with many aspects of the form picture, it can pay to take the idea a bit further and get to know particular characteristics of individual courses. For example, some horses specialise on all-weather surfaces, and since there are only three tracks for them to run on, consistent winners are bound to run up big totals at those courses. But be aware that the two surfaces used for all-weather racing are significantly different, and few horses act so well on the one as on the other. Equitrack, in use at Lingfield Park, is a far quicker surface than the Fibresand of Southwell and Wolverhampton, and much more conducive to pace. Fibresand is a much more demanding surface.

Naturally the more unusual courses are more likely to produce specialists, but bear in mind that form at such tracks should not necessarily be taken at face value when analysing racing at another course. For a variety of reasons, form at Chester often does not work out elsewhere. One is that the very tight shape of the course makes the draw there a crucial element. Additionally, it seems to be the case that Chester favours what might be termed 'dodgy' horses, the type whose attention wanders on, say, the wide expanses of Newmarket but whose interest is engaged by the hurly-burly of racing round the Roodeye. Another characteristic of Chester is that finishing distances become exaggerated, a factor to be taken into account when assessing form there. Over jumps, a similar situation applies on the Mildmay Course at Aintree.

As at Chester, races tend to be run at a very fast pace – resulting in many of the fields finishing noticeably stretched.

Do not assume that stamina necessarily counts for less at a tight track. Even though its circuit is barely a mile round, leading trainer Barry Hills is convinced that a horse really needs to get the trip at Chester. Furthermore, Barry's record at the course more than suggests that he knows what he's talking about!

Over jumps, take into account the known severity of steeplechase fences at particular courses. At Fontwell the fences are considered soft, so the form of a horse running well there and then going on to Newbury, where they are much stiffer, might be treated with caution.

Don't get carried away by the sheer logic of the idea of horses for courses. Remember that horses lose as well as win at their favoured tracks.

Time – know what you're doing, or keep well clear!

For the average everyday punter, the advice so far as the time of races is concerned is straightforward: either leave it alone completely, or immerse yourself in it thoroughly. Stick to what you are comfortable with. If you're comfortable with the use of adjusted race times, you're probably an expert anyway!

Basically, time students – who often use differing methods towards the same end – seek to establish a standard against which individual performances on a given racing day may be measured, providing yet another piece in the mosaic of form.

A method for establishing a race-by-race time comparison at an individual meeting is as follows. Divide the number of furlongs of each race into 100, and express this as pounds: thus each furlong in a five-furlong race is worth twenty pounds, in a one-mile race twelve and a half pounds, in a two-mile race six and a quarter pounds. Say a race over each distance that day is won by a five-year-old carrying ten stone, and all these winners record a time one second better than standard for that course. Which, in terms of time performance, is the best? Answer: the winner of the two-mile race, who has posted a result nearly fourteen pounds better than the five-furlong winner (twenty less six and a quarter equals nearly fourteen). Our example, of course, is simplistic – deliberately so; as in open-aged races, times have to be adjusted to the weight-for-age scale, and so on.

Remember: know what you're doing, or steer clear!

Be open-minded

If a horse runs badly and there is a good excuse, give it another chance. But if you don't know why it ran badly, leave it alone. Sure, you'll miss the odd winner, but you'll save yourself countless losers. Serious value can be had from forgiving one poor run when the reasons are not hard to find. Take 1998 Oaks winner Shahtoush. She ran a blinder when second to Cape Verdi in the One Thousand Guineas at Newmarket over one mile, a trip which her breeding suggested would be on the sharp side for her. She was then a big disappointment when only tenth in the Irish One Thousand Guineas. But that race came soon after her exertions in the Newmarket Classic; the ground at the Curragh was unsuitably fast for her and she experienced traffic problems when trying to make her run. Forgiving sorts who knew she was a top-class filly – her run behind Cape Verdi proved that – and was bred to be even better over the longer distance at Epsom had their faith rewarded when she swooped late under Mick Kinane to land the Oaks at 12–1.

Consider the distance of the race

Keep an eye out for horses moving up in distance, especially those noted as running on well towards the end of a shorter race. In many cases horses like this need further.

According to John Francome, who knows more about such matters than most, by teaching a horse to relax in his races you can develop his stamina. Don't necessarily equate stamina on the Flat with stamina over the same trip over jumps. A miler on the Flat will commonly get twice as far when switched to racing over obstacles – where a vital factor is the brief respite the horse gets from the act of jumping. Crossing twelve fences in a two-mile chase adds up to almost five seconds of relief from the arduous business of galloping, and two miles over jumps is much easier to get than two miles on the Flat.

Another hint: don't take the form in two-mile 'bumpers' – National Hunt Flat Races – as an indication of equal merit with form over the same trip on the Flat; many horses that run in – and win – bumpers do not truly stay the distance. Mary Reveley's old gelding Mellottie was a fine example: he won bumpers over two miles and thirteen furlongs, but, on the Flat, was in his element over a much shorter trip, winning the nine-furlong Cambridgeshire in 1991.

Don't treat weight with slide-rule precision

The weight which a horse carries in a race is naturally very important, but it is just one of a number of factors. Be aware what the weight carried in a handicap indicates: is the horse improving or declining?

To many punters, the weight-for-age scale is one of the more boring aspects of form, but any punter should be aware of what it means and should have access to it (which is why we've given you both the Flat and the jumps versions on pages 180–3). The scale is a tried and tested method of bringing generations together, an official assessment of how far an average young horse is behind his elders in terms of maturity. The knack with, say, an improving three-year-old running against older horses is to catch him as he starts to thrive. On many occasions such types are able to defy the differences laid down in the scale and are capable of beating their elders.

Follow stables in form

Following in-form trainers and avoiding out-of-form yards will enhance the success of your betting considerably, both by pointing you towards winners and by helping you steer clear of losers. Of course, it never works out completely – an out-of-form stable can still send out the odd winner – but it pays to keep a close eye on a trainer's form.

Pay particular attention to the big yards – which have such fire-power that they should be having winners on a regular basis – and to notable small yards.

Try to gauge the crucial period: catch trainers as they come out of the doldrums, and be quickly aware when they are going back in. A fairly obvious warning sign is when a big yard sends out a handful of disappointing runners.

Know your courses

Study the plan of the track. On courses where the runners go into a bend shortly after the start, the draw is almost certainly a crucial factor, with those drawn on the inside at an advantage.

Be aware of how going can affect the draw. In straight races at Newcastle or Thirsk, for example, high numbers (stands rail) are usually favoured – unless the going is soft, when the advantage generally rests with the low numbers (far rail). In neither case is a draw in the middle of a large field an advantage.

Races as form guides

The merit of a race can be gauged by how many horses go on from it to show improvement – measured, for example, through their official handicap ratings – and can only be gained through hindsight and a good deal of cross-referencing. If you are trying to assess the class of a maiden race where the runners have no previous form, a helpful pointer can be the time of the race, compared with that of others on the day.

When did the horse last run – and how far has he travelled?

Whether a long lay-off reflects adversely on a horse's chance depends entirely on the individual: some need time between their races, some thrive on running frequently.

Take particular note of sprinters: they can hit 'seams' of form in which they run frequently and can hold their form for several races over a short period of time. Once a good handicap sprinter gets into that seam, follow him. During such a spell the horse may be running off his old official handicap mark (see page 51) before being reassessed, but don't get too fussy over ratings: if the horse in question is fit and well, running at the top of his form, and on his ideal ground, a pound or two in weight is not going to make much difference.

Some punters pay a great deal of attention to how far a horse has travelled to take part in the race, but as with so many elements of the form picture, this issue has to be approached sensibly. The majority of owners want runners at the big meetings. So, that a horse has travelled a long way to get to Cheltenham in March is unlikely to be of great significance. However, pay special attention to horses driven extreme distances to lesser meetings – especially from smaller yards. If John Dunlop sends a horse from Arundel to Pontefract, the fact is unlikely to go unnoticed by punters. But when a small trainer sends a horse on a very long journey to run, it's often for a significant opportunity.

First-time blinkers

Be more wary of first-time blinkers when fitted to stayers. With sprinters, they often give a horse an edge – that ability really to focus on the race – which can make all the difference.

Always be on the look-out for value

Exactly what constitutes 'value' for the punter is a subjective matter, but here's an example. Take a big field of handicappers.

You look at the race with a view to picking the winner, and you find five horses with a real chance: it's difficult to divide them. If you take under 4–1 about any of those you need your head examining. But say one of them is on offer at 8–1 or more – win or lose, that's value. It's as simple as that: a horse represents value when the odds on offer are longer than you think reflect his chance. If you constantly back horses which are bad value, in the long term you will lose.

Market moves

Always assess betting moves within the context of the course market. A major move at a big meeting – the Cheltenham Festival, say, or Royal Ascot – is much more significant than at a small one, where crowds are sparse and it takes very little off-course money to manipulate the market.

Be wary of letting market moves put you off a selection you've made on grounds of form, the appearance of the horse, etc., and only be dissuaded from your original choice if the vibes in the betting ring are so bad they can't be ignored.

Try to leave placing your bet as late as possible

It's difficult to keep an eye on movements in the betting ring and get a good look at the horses, but if you're at the course you can gain an impression of a horse's well-being by studying him in the pre-parade ring – and then, if you like what you see, nip off to the ring to get on.

• • •

When you've taken on board all of the above, remember that the golden rule for all punters, the piece of advice to have etched not just on the first page of your form book but deep into the front cover, is ...

When in doubt, stay out!

Successful betting is as much about not backing losers as about backing winners. Never chase your losses. There is always another day.

The form factors

Sean Magee

A three-horse race brings together three two-year-old colts – Angelic, Buttercup and Cowpat.

Each horse has run once before: Angelic and Buttercup in the same race, against Dunderhead (who is not running today), and Cowpat in a different race against Dunderhead. In their first race, over five furlongs on good going, Angelic and Buttercup carried the same weight and dead-heated to share second place, a length behind Dunderhead, who also carried the same weight. Today Angelic carries three pounds more than Buttercup and two pounds more than Cowpat. On the 'direct' form of the previous race against each other, Buttercup should this time finish in front of Angelic, as he now has a weight advantage. But 'collateral' form through another horse highlights the chance of Cowpat, as he beat Dunderhead a length at level weights when they met, whereas Angelic and Buttercup finished behind Dunderhead. Yes, but today's race is over seven furlongs, not five, and Angelic is bred for stamina. And today the going is heavy, not good, and Buttercup's dam liked soft going. Furthermore, Buttercup looked very burly in the parade ring before that race, and should be fitter today. Then again, Buttercup's trainer hasn't had a winner for six weeks . . .

Form is fact. The skill lies in its interpretation, and in weighing the comparative importance of the different elements which go to make up the complete form picture. Those key elements are:

Distance of the race

Although some horses are genuinely versatile in terms of distance, most have an ideal trip or range of trips. What that ideal is will not necessarily be obvious until the horse has run a few times. To take an example from a couple of years ago, the four-year-old gelding Sandbaggedagain, trained by Mick Easterby, started the 1998 Flat season running over seven furlongs, though his only victory as a three-year-old had been over a mile and a half. After three unsuccessful outings at seven furlongs he was moved up to a mile and a quarter and started to find a little form; he stepped up to twelve furlongs on his next two outings and continued to run creditably without winning – then moved yet further up in distance to two miles and hit a winning vein, landing a handicap at Catterick before going on to take the Brown Jack Stakes at Ascot.

First indications of a horse's optimum distance lie with its breeding, as stamina, like speed, is hereditary – up to a point. There are plenty of examples of a horse's ability to last out an extended trip going against the evidence of its breeding, none more remarkable than the case of Red Rum. Three times he won the longest race in the calendar, the Grand National over four and a half miles (and for good measure was runner-up in the Aintree marathon on two other occasions), yet his sire Quorum never won at a distance beyond a mile.

Or take the case of King's Best, whose explosive burst of speed landed him the Two Thousand Guineas in 2000. Once it was announced that his target after that Classic victory over one mile would be the Derby over half as long again, his chance at Epsom seemed to revolve principally around the issue of whether he would stay the mile and a half. For weeks the debate raged. His sire Kingmambo never won beyond a mile but his dam Allegretta showed good form at a mile and a half, so on breeding there were grounds for optimism about King's Best's ability to last the Derby trip. What undermined such a view was his style of winning the Guineas, as it is rare for a horse to combine depth of stamina with the ability to quicken in such an immediate manner. Sadly we were never to know whether King's Best would stay a mile and half or not – he missed Epsom and broke down in the Irish Derby – but the debate about his stamina was characteristic of one of the trickiest elements of form study.

A couple of years earlier much of the build-up to the Derby was centred on the potential stamina of another leading contender, One Thousand Guineas winner Cape Verdi. Her pedigree appeared to offer grounds for optimism. Her sire Caerleon had won the Prix du Jockey-Club over a mile and a half and had already sired a Derby winner in Generous; her dam Afrique Bleu Azur had won over eleven and a half furlongs in France, and was a daughter of Sagace, winner of the Prix de l'Arc de Triomphe over a mile and a half. On pedigree, it seemed reasonable to assume Cape Verdi would stay. Unlike King's Best, Cape Verdi actually made the Epsom line-up, and, as so often, it took the race to settle the point: the filly faded inside the final quarter mile – a telling indication that she had failed to last the trip.

The moral is simple. Racecourse performance is always the most reliable indicator of any aspect of form – and the corollary of that is that the more form a horse has, the fuller picture you build of him and the less you need to rely on guesswork and theory.

A word of warning, though: assessing that performance is not so simple. Several factors affect how far a particular performance testifies to a horse's stamina – the pace at which a race was run, the state of the going, the nature of the track – and these must be weighed up and interpreted. For instance, any horse which is staying on at the end of a truly run race over two miles at Newmarket in soft going may reasonably be assumed to 'get the trip' – that is, last out the full distance – whereas the winner of a slowly run race over two miles on firm going around a much tighter and flatter track such as Folkestone could not – on that evidence alone – be said to have the same degree of stamina.

The question of stamina is rarely clear-cut. Some experts think that the Derby course of a mile and a half can suit a horse which truly stays no more than a mile and a quarter, as more of it is downhill than uphill: Sir Ivor in 1968 is one example of a horse who won the Derby but whose performance elsewhere showed that his preferred trip was only one and a quarter miles.

Going

Of all the factors that can influence the performance of a racehorse the going is generally the most critical. Only a small proportion of the racehorse population can be said to 'act on any going'; some horses are much more effective with give in the ground (lightly-made individuals with comparatively little body-weight to lift out of the ground often seem to be well suited by a soft surface); others are particularly well suited by firm going. The outcome of nearly every race is influenced to some extent by the state of the ground, the influence sometimes being to a marked degree.

As an expression of the importance of the state of the racing surface as a factor in form study, that extract from the entry on Mr Frisk in Timeform's *Chasers and Hurdlers 1989–90* could hardly be bettered. And Mr Frisk himself could hardly be bettered as an example of a horse whose performance was transformed by a particular state of the ground. In fast conditions he was brilliant, but the softer the going, the more ordinary he became – not an ideal trait for a steeplechaser, for whom most opportunities take place in the soft ground of the winter months. But when in 1990 the Grand National going was officially firm for the first time since 1961 – Nicolaus Silver's year – Mr Frisk found himself in his element, winning the National in a time which knocked a staggering fourteen seconds off the previous record for the race set by Red Rum in 1973. And for good measure Mr Frisk went on the following month to land the Whitbread Gold Cup in similar conditions.

At the other end of the going spectrum was another Grand National victor, Earth Summit, who just outstayed the heroic Suny Bay in desperately heavy ground in 1998. Earth Summit had won the Welsh National earlier the same season in similarly extreme conditions, and the fact that he was proven to be able to act in such a quagmire lay behind the gamble which brought him down to favouritism at Aintree.

Physical traits – conformation and action – influence a probable suitability for extremes of ground. The Timeform quotation above makes the point about light-framed horses preferring soft ground, and it is sometimes said that a horse with large feet will also like the mud, since a larger foot has more grip.

As important as size alone is the horse's action, the way it moves. Watch the runners as they canter to post. A horse with a 'round' action – one which brings its knees high in each stride – is likely to go well on soft or muddy going, while the animal with a more economical 'daisy-cutting' stride, where the feet seem to be lifted over the ground only just far enough to clear it, will probably find the soft less suitable, and act more effectively on fast ground. A horse that seems to 'float' elegantly over the ground on good going may well get stuck in the soft.

Clearly, if a horse appears to have a distinct preference for a particular state of going, its chances will be affected by the weather. Having the 'wrong' ground does not, of course, mean that the horse categorically will not win, but it does mean that he is unlikely to run to his best form.

In any race, no assessment of the runners' chances is complete that does not take into account the likely effect of the going. While most horses should be able to act effectively on good ground, when extremes occur – very hard or very heavy – always pay serious attention to horses who have won or run well on similar going in the past.

Going

Formal description of the state of the going at a race meeting is the responsibility of the Clerk of the Course, who announces the probable going some time in advance to advise trainers about likely conditions, then provides regular updates. On the day of the meeting he or she declares the official state of the going (which can alter during the course of the afternoon's racing, say in the case of torrential rain).

The seven official states of the going in Britain for races on turf are:

hard; firm; good to firm; good; good to soft; soft; heavy.

The official states of the going for all-weather races are:

fast; standard; slow.

Like so many aspects of racing, the state of the going is often discussed in a jargon which may seem baffling to newcomers. Here's a short glossary:

'top of the ground': firm, fast going
'bottomless': very heavy
'cut in the ground': on the soft side of good
'lively': on the firm side
'a sound surface': not too soft
'getting his toe in': on the soft side

Class

All form is relative to the class of the event in which it is recorded; so it is important to know the standard of each race you are contemplating when building up a picture of form. Fifth place in a Classic represents a much better performance than victory in a lowly race (though how far was the fifth horse behind the winner?). Information about the class of a race is easily gained from the detailed form in the racing press (see 'Sources of Information', pages 54–63), which will give the prize money and level of the past race in question.

- On the Flat, there are six classifications, from Class A (Pattern and Listed races – that is, the cream of the year's events) down to Class G (selling races with small amounts of prize money, and apprentice and amateur races of similar value).
- Over jumps, there are seven ranks, from Class A (races run under the jumping Pattern) down to Class H (hunter-chases and National Hunt Flat Races – 'bumpers' – of low value).

You do not need to know the exact definition of each class, but you do need to be aware that form in a Class B race is likely to be of a significantly higher standard than form in a Class F race.

Whatever the race, the worth of the form becomes established as horses that took part appear again – either (to use jargon) 'franking' or 'advertising' the form or running poorly ('devaluing') it. Gradually a picture of the overall quality of the race is built up. Take, for example, the 2000 Vodafone Derby won by Sinndar. The winner, who went on to land the Irish Derby and the Prix de l'Arc de Triomphe, was undeniably a horse of the highest class, but what of the overall class of the Derby itself? Or, to use the racing idiom, how did the form hold up? The bare bones of the subsequent form of each runner in Sinndar's Derby reads as follows:

	horse	*runs*	*wins*
1	Sinndar	3	3 (two Group 1, one Group 2)
2	Sakhee	1	0
3	Beat Hollow	1	1 (Group 1)
4	Best Of The Bests	4	1 (Group 2)
5	Wellbeing	2	2 (one Group 3)
6	Hatha Anna	1	0
7	St Expedit	3	0
8	Barathea Guest	6	0
9	Zyz	2	0
10	Aristotle	0	0
11	Inchlonaig	0	0
12	Broche	0	0
13	Going Global	5	0
14	Cracow	5	1
15	Kingsclere	2	0

So between them the runners in the 2000 Derby ran thirty-five more races that year and managed just eight wins. Admittedly the winner was a top-class performer; but of those behind Sinndar only Beat Hollow won a Group One race, and the ten horses who finished sixth or worse at Epsom managed a solitary win between them – Cracow in a handicap at York.

What does that suggest to you about the *overall* quality of that Derby field?

Hindsight is a great factor in the study of form: make use of it. In your form book, go through the previous races of each day's winners and mark them off: the form of a heavily marked event is clearly working out well. Such a trend may point you towards horses yet to race. If the form is standing up, those horses are worth looking for.

Time

The study and use of race times can be immensely complicated, and most casual punters have only a vague notion of how important an element of form the matter of time can be, generally leaving it to the time experts in the racing press to tell them what is significant.

Compared with human athletes, horses have not, as a whole, got much faster over the last fifty years. But though record times themselves are not considered especially important, the comparison of the times that different horses take to win different races over the same course can be very significant – it is worth noting that many of the top professional backers consider the study of race times one of the most significant weapons in their battle against the bookmakers – and it was to facilitate such comparisons that the concept of the standard time was introduced. The standard time on the Flat is a time for each distance at each course adjusted to a horse carrying nine stone on good or firm ground, and is calculated by taking the average of the ten fastest runnings. Courses vary hugely, as standard times reflect. At the beginning of 2000 the Raceform standard time over five furlongs at Epsom was 54.2 seconds;

at Sandown Park, with its stiff uphill finish, the standard time for the same trip was 1 minute 0.2 seconds. The time of the winning horse will be given in relation to standard, 'above' meaning slower than standard, 'below' faster.

The advantage of race times is that they constitute a completely objective body of evidence which can be used to compare the abilities of horses who have never raced against each other. However, remember that the evidence of the clock must be tempered by other considerations. Was the race run at a true pace? Was it run at the end of a day when heavy rain throughout the programme might have changed the going? Was the winner pushed out to the line or was he easing up? As with every aspect of form, all these details need to be factored in – which brings us back to the experts in the racing papers and form services, who do the maths and come up with ratings based on time.

Course

You can do a lot worse than follow the notion of 'horses for courses' when trying to pick a winner, especially on notoriously quirky tracks such as Chester, Epsom or Windsor. Any horse running on a course where it has won before is worthy of consideration, for it is clearly able to act effectively on that track; exactly how much importance you attach to such evidence depends on both horse and course. Remember, too, that while all British racecourses are different, many have aspects in common, and it pays to know something of the nature of each track: is it right-handed or left-handed, is it flat or undulating, galloping or tight? By familiarising yourself with the intricacies, you will become better equipped to judge

Five horses for five courses

- Tempering won twenty-two races on the all-weather track at Southwell
- Rapporteur won nineteen times at Lingfield Park – fourteen times on the all-weather track
- Suluk won eighteen races at Southwell (all-weather again)
- Manhattan Boy won fourteen races at Plumpton
- Rapid Lad won twelve races at Beverley

whether the horse you saw scoot home in a three-mile chase at Kempton is likely to find the same trip at Cheltenham equally suitable.

Trainer and jockey

When a stable is on a roll, it pays to follow it.

The trick, of course, is cottoning on to this when the yard is coming to the boil, not when the winning streak is petering out. The racing press gives detailed information about which trainers are in good form, and about which have especially good records at particular courses, and these statistics can be invaluable: see pages 184–99.

Conversely, when a stable has hit a thin patch, you would be well advised to be very wary of its runners until its form picks up. Poor form by a particular yard is often caused by a virus affecting the horses, which does not become apparent until they run: in these circumstances it is very difficult to support a horse sent out by that trainer with any confidence, and whatever the attractions of his form on paper, the punter does best to be wary, bearing in mind the theory that it is better to miss a winner than back a loser – though while the advice is incontrovertible on the grounds that it costs you nothing in monetary terms to see the horse you were going to back romp home, the emotional anguish can be severe.

Jockeys, too, have purple patches, and a winning run can do wonders for a rider's confidence, lending the pilot an assurance that flows down the reins and galvanises the horse. Always pay attention to a jockey hitting a seam of form. And note who has ridden a horse in previous races: if for the current race Eddery or Dettori is taking the ride on a runner usually partnered by an apprentice or a lesser-known rider, that could be significant. Look out, too, for a top jockey who has gone to an obscure meeting to ride for an unfashionable stable: he will not have done so simply for the

The most spectacular example of a jockey hitting a purple patch is of course Frankie Dettori's Magnificent Seven at Ascot on 28 September 1996, when he rode the winners of all seven races: Wall Street (2–1), Diffident (12–1), Mark Of Esteem (100–30), Decorated Hero (7–1), Fatefully (7–4), Lochangel (5–4) and Fujiyama Crest (2–1)

Had you thought beforehand that Frankie might be in for a good day and backed those seven as a £1 sevenfold accumulator, you would have won £25,095.

pleasure of a drive in the country. And in particular, pay heed to which jockeys do noticeably well at those tracks considered particularly difficult to ride – Epsom, say, or Bath or Catterick. The papers will give you a list of top jockeys there over the last few years, and these lists always repay close study.

Interpretation of the effect of the draw can be a contentious business.

In September 2000 the twenty-three-runner Milcars Ruislip Handicap over five furlongs at Kempton Park looked like a race dominated by the draw, with many experts convinced that runners drawn low – the side nearer the stands – were at a marked disadvantage, so marked that on *The Morning Line* that day Barry Dennis offered generous odds against any of the low-drawn horses finishing in the first four.

What happened?

The stands side provided the first six home at hefty prices:

	horse	*draw*	*SP*
1	Candleriggs	3	25–1
2	Ivory Dawn	1	33–1
3	Lone Piper	6	40–1
4	Literary Society	7	33–1
5	Cadeaux Cher	10	20–1
6	Pedro Jack	2	25–1

So much for the experts ...

Draw

In races on the Flat over less than a mile, the draw – the allocation of each runner to the numbered stall from which it will start – can have a crucial effect on a horse's chance, although over longer distances its influence is usually considerably less. The effect of the draw is much more marked at some courses than others: at certain courses in some conditions a horse with a particular draw might have a negligible chance – in which case, while you might not want to back it that time, a prominent run is possibly more meritorious than it appears at face value. So always note the draw in races which are building up the form picture, for it will have a bearing on how you interpret the result.

The betting market

For each horse taking part in a race, the form published in the racing press will include a summary of how the odds offered about that runner altered between the time betting opened on the event and the start of the race. This information can be highly revealing, for a horse whose odds shorten is being backed, while one whose odds lengthen is attracting less money – and these indications about confidence behind a horse, or the lack of it, constitute another piece in the form mosaic.

As a simple example, take the six-furlong Class F handicap on the all-weather surface at Southwell on 12 February 2001, as humdrum a race as you could wish for. Forecast 100–30 favourite in that morning's *Racing Post* was Raayeh, with Pawn In Life one of the less fancied contenders at a predicted 8–1.

continued on page 46

The effect of the draw

It is impossible to be dogmatic about the effect of the draw on a particular course, since several factors can affect which side is favoured. This course-by-course list sums up the generally regarded opinion of the draw factor at all thirty-four Flat courses in Britain.

Ascot

Low numbers favoured on the straight course in soft going.

Ayr

High numbers favoured in big fields on the straight course, especially when the going is soft.

Bath

Apparently little effect, though the five-furlong course here is on a gradual left-hand bend which might be thought to favour low numbers.

Beverley

High numbers noticeably favoured in five-furlong races.

Brighton

Low numbers favoured in sprint races, but high numbers when the going is soft.

Carlisle

High numbers seem to have an advantage in races up to one mile.

Catterick

Over five furlongs, low numbers appear to be favoured except when the ground is soft, when high numbers seem to have an advantage; over six and seven furlongs, low numbers are favoured.

Chepstow

No marked advantage either side.

Chester

Low numbers appear to be favoured, but the crucial factor here is a quick break, irrespective of draw.

Doncaster

Low numbers used to have a noticeable advantage in big fields on the straight course when the going is soft, but the effect is becoming increasingly difficult to predict.

Epsom Downs

High numbers strongly favoured over five furlongs, less so over six furlongs.

Folkestone

High numbers favoured in sprint races.

Goodwood

Little effect.

Haydock Park

High numbers favoured in sprints, especially when the going is soft.

Kempton Park

On the sprint course, a high number is advantageous when the stalls are on the far side (especially in softer ground), a low number when the stalls are on the stands side.

Leicester

Middle to high numbers favoured on the straight course.

The effect of the draw (continued)

Lingfield Park

Low numbers slightly favoured in sprints on the all-weather course; on the turf course high numbers appear to be favoured.

Musselburgh

High numbers favoured in five-furlong races when stalls on the stands side, high numbers when stalls on the far side.

Newbury

No advantage.

Newcastle

On the straight course, horses drawn towards either rail seem to have an advantage; when the going is soft, low numbers are especially favoured.

Newmarket

Little significant advantage over any distance on either the Rowley Mile or the July Course.

Nottingham

High numbers favoured in sprint races when stalls on stands side, low numbers when stalls on far side.

Pontefract

Low numbers favoured in sprint races.

Redcar

Middle to high numbers slightly favoured on the straight course.

Ripon
Low numbers appear favoured on the straight course.

Salisbury
Low numbers tend to be favoured in sprint races on soft going.

Sandown Park
On the five-furlong course, high numbers have an advantage when the ground is soft and when the stalls are placed on the far side; low numbers are favoured when the stalls are on the stands side.

Southwell
No advantage in straight five furlongs; low draw favoured over six and seven furlongs.

Thirsk
Significant advantage for high numbers on the straight course, more pronounced when the ground is fast.

Warwick
Low numbers favoured in shorter races except when the going is soft – in which case the stands side tends to run faster.

Windsor
High numbers favoured in sprints.

Wolverhampton
Low numbers favoured in sprints.

Yarmouth
High numbers slightly favoured on the straight course.

York
Little effect either way.

The betting report for this race speaks volumes about their respective prospects as the market fluctuated in the few minutes leading up to the off. Raayeh opened at 11–4 market leader, then drifted out to a starting price of nearly twice those odds, 5–1. Meanwhile Pawn In Life had opened at 5–1 (8–1 in one place), momentarily eased to 6–1, and was then the subject of significant backing, his odds rapidly shrinking until he became 3–1 favourite. Had you been following these moves, you would have deduced that Pawn In Life was well fancied and Raayeh was not – an assessment confirmed in the race itself: Pawn In Life won and landed the gamble, while Raayeh finished well down the field.

The running of the race

A key element in the form picture of any horse is a brief description of how it ran in each race recorded. Was it running on at the finish (in which case it has no stamina problems, and might need a longer trip)? Was it able to accelerate? Did it make the pace, or come from last to first? Did it encounter problems in running which might explain an otherwise unexpectedly poor finishing position? The comments given in the form are for the most part bald and factual – the closest the writers ever get to overt enthusiasm is 'won easily' – but from the depressingly straightforward 'always behind, tailed off' or 'never near enough to challenge' to the equally straightforward 'never headed', these laconic comments will tell you a lot about the way the horse fared.

A particular pointer to future performance can be 'ran on well'. Win or lose, the horse described thus was still racing right up to the line.

Time since last race

Recent form is the best form; indeed, many shrewd punters will not back a horse when its form, however good, dates from a period too long before the current race. But sometimes old form is all one has – notably, of course, on a horse's seasonal debut. With horses that race for season after season, it pays to be aware of whether they tend to need a run or two to get to their top form, or whether they are usually ready to do themselves justice first time out.

Most newspapers print alongside each runner in each event the number of days since the horse last raced: a horse that has not run for a very long time could well be rusty and need this race to make it fit. But punters who turned against Derby runners Lammtarra in 1995 and Shaamit in 1996 on the grounds that they had not had a previous race that season would have had cause to rue their prejudice: Lammtarra won the premier Classic at 14–1, and Shaamit at 12–1.

In April 2000 Mely Moss very nearly pulled off the even more extraordinary feat of winning the Grand National without a previous run that season, only giving best to Papillon shortly before the post. Before that herculean effort, Mely Moss had not run for 346 days.

But do not get carried away if a horse turns in a good performance on its first run following a long lay-off. It is often the case that the run after that one shows a significant decline in form.

Weight

You've studied everything about the runners, and picked your fancy: he's done a good time over this distance, he loves the course, the going is just right for him, his jockey is flying, his trainer can do no wrong – but if he's carrying two stone more than the best of his rivals, you'd have to think again.

In the Classics, all horses carry the same weight (except for an allowance to fillies in the Two Thousand Guineas, Derby and St Leger), so weight is not an element in assessing the likely outcome. The same is true of the premier National Hunt races. But in many other races there are discrepancies in the weights carried that must be taken into account. In 'weight-for-age' races, these discrepancies are calculated to counterbalance the advantage that a more mature horse will have over a younger rival: the weight-for-age scale (pages 180–3) lays down the officially designated differences for horses of different ages over different distances at different times of the year. Naturally the effect of weight variations will not be the same at all distances: if a horse is beaten a neck in a five-furlong sprint he will theoretically dead-heat with his conqueror next time they meet if he carries one pound less weight; in a three-mile steeplechase a pound is generally regarded as worth a length.

The effect of weight is most marked, of course, in handicaps: races in which the runners are allotted different weights to render their chances theoretically equal. Handicapping is an inexact activity, and you need to be aware of this when assessing the performance of runners in this type of event: more credence can be given to the distances separating the first three or four home than the distances between the stragglers. Often, too, a horse will win easily but not by very far: alert observers will make due allowances.

Remember that a horse running 'out of the handicap' does not appear to have a good chance at the weights. A horse is 'out of the handicap' if under the terms of that race he has to carry a weight greater than he was originally allotted in relation to the horse carrying the highest weight in the race.

A brief rule of thumb for relating weight to finishing distances is:

Flat

- 5 furlongs to 7 furlongs: 3 pounds per length
- 1 mile to 11 furlongs: 2 pounds per length
- 1½ miles to 2 miles: 1½ pounds per length
- over 2 miles: 1 pound per length

jumps

- 1 pound per length (though make downward adjustments for extreme distances)

First-time blinkers

The purpose of fitting blinkers on a horse for a race is to get him to concentrate on the business in hand by focusing his sight to the front, rather than allowing him to be distracted by goings-on in his lateral field of vision. Some horses become wise to this ploy and get used to the blinkers, thus minimising their effect, so the first run wearing them can produce a significant improvement in form. Don't think of blinkers as an indication of an irresolute nature – the manner in which the blinkered Earth Summit won the 1998 Grand National in desperate going was evidence of the doughtiest spirit – and there have been plenty of cases of perfectly genuine horses regularly running in blinkers: they just get easily distracted, and need to have their attention focused on the job in hand.

Distance travelled to racecourse

On the basis that, say, an inmate of Martin Pipe's yard making the 377-mile journey from his stable in Nicholashayne in Devon to the racecourse at Ayr would not be doing so for a relaxing drive up the motorway, some form experts pay great attention to horses who have been sent a significantly long way to race. The *Racing Post* provides a list of such runners for each day.

First run for a new trainer

Many horses benefit from a change of scene, and a move from one trainer to another can be significant. Whether it heralds a marked improvement in performance tends to depend on who he's left and who he's joined!

To repeat: form is fact – a mass of fact. What you have to do is learn how to read, interpret and use all the strands in that mass of fact, and to add to it the magic extra ingredient of your own opinion. Remember that form only takes you up to the last performance. To come to your final assessment of the horses' chances, it must be accompanied by your judgement of the runners' condition before the race.

And don't forget that the same mass of fact is also available to the bookmakers!

• • •

Ratings

Every horse in training, once it has run often enough to be assessed, is given an official rating by the handicappers of the British Horseracing Board, in the range

- on the Flat: 0–140;
- over jumps: 0–175.

Each point on this scale is equivalent to a pound in weight: that is, Horse A, rated 121, is deemed to be one pound 'better' than Horse B, rated 120, which in turn means that were they to race against one another with Horse A carrying nine stone two pounds and Horse B carrying nine stone one pound, they should theoretically dead-heat.

The official rating is revised every week, going up or down or staying the same depending both on how the horse has performed and on whether a race in which he has run has proved to be of better quality than originally considered. So, should a horse win off a particular rating, or 'mark', and there is time to run again before he is rehandicapped – that is, his official rating is revised – connections may well be tempted to give him another race during that period if a suitable opportunity arises. In some cases a penalty – an additional weight to be carried if the horse has won a race since the last revision – will apply to take account of the improvement not yet reflected in the official ratings.

So when you hear a Channel Four pundit refer to a horse having 'won off 99', and relating that to his current mark, he or she is referring to the horse's official rating. And reference to a '0–90 handicap' means a handicap for horses rated no higher than 90.

As an example of how official ratings are revised to reflect improvement in a horse, consider the case of Lady Rockstar, the Mick Ryan-trained filly whose sequence of eight wins in a row in less than five weeks was a feature of the early part of the 1998 Flat season. When she started her winning run she was rated a very lowly 41, and then . . .

28 May	won at Ayr off 41
3 June	won at Folkestone off 46
5 June	won at Haydock, still off 46
11 June	won at Yarmouth off 53
17 June	won at Nottingham off 62
22 June	won at Windsor off 70
26 June	won at Folkestone off 71
29 June	won at Windsor off 73
8 July	unplaced at Newmarket off 84

. . . and her rating for future races had been increased to 89 by the time of that Newmarket appearance.

A recent example of a jumper taking a ratings hike is Jonjo O'Neill's good chaser Legal Right in the 1999–2000 season:

9 October	pulled up at Bangor-on-Dee off 119
14 November	won at Cheltenham off 115

26 November   won at Newbury off 126
11 December   won Tripleprint Gold Cup at Cheltenham off 134

Timeform's top ratings

On the Flat, the highest annual ratings awarded by Timeform to horses who raced in Britain since the Second World War are:

145 Sea Bird II (1965)
144 Brigadier Gerard (1972), Tudor Minstrel (1947)
142 Abernant (1949), Ribot (1956), Windy City (1951)
141 Mill Reef (1972)
140 Dancing Brave (1986), Dubai Millennium (2000), Shergar (1981), Vaguely Noble (1968)

Over jumps, the highest rated have been:

212 Arkle (1965–6)
210 Flyingbolt (1965–6)
191 Mill House (1963–4)
187 Desert Orchid (1989–90)
186 Dunkirk (1965–6)
184 Burrough Hill Lad (1984–5)
183 Master Oats (1994–5)
182 Captain Christy (1975–6), Carvill's Hill (1991–2), Night Nurse (1976–7)
180 Monksfield (1978–9)

After that Cheltenham victory (his final outing that season) he was raised to 150, off which mark he won the Tote Silver Cup at Ascot in December 2000, occasioning yet another big increase, to 163.

Apart from the official BHB ratings, some newspapers publish their own private handicaps; these will be broadly similar to the official list but may include some significantly different assessments, according to how each individual pundit interprets the form. Best known and most widely consulted of the unofficial ratings are those provided by Timeform, who maintain a running handicap of every horse in training throughout the season.

• • •

Sources of information

The official form book, published by Raceform on behalf of the British Horseracing Board and available in weekly or twice-weekly instalments, provides extensive details of every race run in Great Britain as well as the major races overseas (see pages 62–3). Beyond the official form book, there are several sources of information, some more elaborate than others.

The *Racing Post* – since the demise of the *Sporting Life* in May 1998 the only daily racing newspaper in Britain – includes very extensive and sophisticated statistics. A detailed run-down of the form of every runner in every race is laid out, along with expert interpretation of that form. Also provided in a mind-boggling array of data are such additional details as the *Post*'s own ratings, and how these relate to the official ratings; trainers' and jockeys' records; statistics regarding the performance of favourites at each of the day's tracks; which horses have travelled furthest to the meetings; and lots more. For surfers of the web, the *Racing Post* is now available free on-line at www.racingpost.co.uk.

The sports pages of the national daily papers print the day's racing programmes, and some offer brief form summaries and related information, while racegoers are usually provided with a three-line form summary for each runner in the racecard. But for specialist information on a daily basis you have to consult the *Racing Post* – or, for the Saturday racing fixtures which for many punters form their main opportunity of the week, the weekly newspaper *Raceform on Saturday*.

Best-known of the private companies that dispense information about racing form is Timeform, based at Halifax in Yorkshire, the largest concern in the world devoted to the publication of form. Timeform produces many publications, notably the annuals *Racehorses* (which lists and discusses every runner on the Flat) and *Chasers and Hurdlers* (for jumpers), and the daily Timeform Racecard, which provides detailed runner-by-runner analysis of every race at every meeting, and rates the chances of each horse according to Timeform's own ratings. (A rating accompanied by the dreaded 'Timeform squiggle' indicates a horse of unreliable temperament.)

If you have neither time nor inclination to sift the data yourself or follow the guidance of newspaper form experts, you can buy the services – and the inside information – of those whose advertisements for telephone tipping lines pepper the pages of the racing press. But it's so much more satisfying to work it all out on your own – and know that your winnings have been earned by the sheer might of your own brain-power.

The card in the *Racing Post* for the Pillar Property Chase at Cheltenham on 27 January 2001.

This is a Grade 2, Class A event over three miles one and a half furlongs, due off at 2.50, fourth race on that afternoon's card, and to be shown live on Channel Four. First prize is £45,000.

The race conditions indicate that the total prize fund for the race is guaranteed to be not less than £75,000; that the race is for six-year-olds and older; that the basic weight each runner is to carry is eleven stone, except that a horse who since 30 September 1999 has won a Class C weight-for-age chase or a Class B handicap will carry a penalty of four pounds (that is, four pounds more than the basic eleven stone), a Class B weight-for-age chase or Class A handicap chase six pounds, and a Class A weight-for-age chase ten pounds; half penalties apply if such wins were in novice chases. Mares have an allowance of five pounds. There were twelve initial entries, whose owners each paid £250 to enter. Penalty value (that is, the winning owner's prize money before mandatory deductions) is £45,000; the owner of the second receives £17,250, third £8,625, fourth £4,125.

See More Business will carry number 1. He was foaled in Ireland ('IRE'); it is thirty-two days since he last ran. He has won over this distance at this course ('CD') and has been a beaten favourite ('BF'); will wear blinkers ('b'), is aged eleven, and in this race carries eleven stone ten pounds; is a bay gelding by Seymour Hicks out of Miss Redlands. He is trained by P. F. Nicholls, is owned by Paul K. Barber and Robert Ogden, and will be ridden by M. A. Fitzgerald. His rating for this race in the *Racing Post*'s Postmark handicap is 192 (the placing of which rating in a solid black disc indicates that he has the highest rating in this race).

The abbreviated form line immediately to the left of See More Business's name shows that he was fifth on his most recent outing and won the one before that. Form before the dash (in this case, 1141) denotes his last four runs the previous season. (Other letters found in the form line include P for pulled up, F for fell, B for brought down, U for unseated rider, R for refused, S for slipped up.)

Cyfor Malta was foaled in France, and did not run at all last season: form before the oblique in his form line denotes the season before last.

There follow brief details of the running of this race in 2000 (winner Looks Like Trouble, trained by Noel Chance and ridden by Norman Williamson, was an eight-year-old carrying eleven stone six pounds who started at 100-30 and won off a Postmark rating of 183).

Beneath the previous result is the betting forecast and Spotlight's runner-by-runner analysis, followed by a summing up of the race (those comments are

2.50 RACE 4

Pillar Property Chase (Class A) (Grade 2) CH4

Winner £45,000 3m1½f New

£75000 guaranteed For 6yo+ **Weights** 11st **Penalties** after September 30th, 1999, a winner of a Class C weight-for-age chase or a Class B handicap chase 4lb; of a Class B w-f-a chase or a Class A handicap chase 6lb; of a Class A w-f-a chase 10lb (half penalties for wins achieved in novice chases in GB/Ireland) **Allowances** mares 5lb **Entries** 12 pay £250 **Penalty value** 1st £45,000 **2nd** £17,250 **3rd** £8,625 **4th** £4,125

1141-15 **SEE MORE BUSINESS** (IRE) 32 b 11 11-10
1 *b g Seymour Hicks-Miss Redlands* **M A FitzGerald** (192)
P F Nicholls Paul K Barber & Robert Ogden

121-3P4 **BEAU** (IRE) 32 8 11-6
2 *b g Zaffaran-Sand Martin* **C Llewellyn** (191)
N A Twiston-Davies Mrs S Tainton

/2121-4 **LORD NOELIE** (IRE) 97 8 11-5
3 *b g Lord Americo-Leallen* **J Culloty** (169)
Miss H C Knight Executive Racing

121111/ **CYFOR MALTA** (FR) 728 8 11-0
4 *b g Cyborg-Force Nine* **A P McCoy** (189)
M C Pipe D A Johnson

2000 (6 ran) **Looks Like Trouble** Noel T Chance 8 11-6 100/30 N Williamson PM193

BETTING FORECAST: 11-8 Cyfor Malta, See More Business, 9-2 Beau, 9 Lord Noelie.

SPOTLIGHT

See More Business Below par in the King George at Kempton last time and possible that, at the age of 11, he is on the verge of decline now; top-class chaser though, winner of the Gold Cup here two years ago, and had looked as good as ever with wide-margin defeat of two good subsequent winners on seasonal debut at Wetherby; very much the one to beat if back in top form, with conditions ideal.

Beau Very useful sound-jumping novice last season, though wide-margin Whitbread win probably flatters him; trip, track and ground no problem but on this season's form, including latest fourth in King George at Kempton, doesn't look good enough against the two principals.

Lord Noelie High-class novice last season, winning the SunAlliance Chase here in March; lightly raced enough to improve further but this soft ground is a negative and has too much to find on overall form to make any great appeal; this season's one run, albeit over an inadequate 2m5f, was well below par.

Cyfor Malta Absent through injury since winning this two years ago (See More Business below form in third) but connections bullish and unlikely to want for fitness; no reason why he shouldn't run to beat under these conditions and, in receipt of 10lb, his old form suggests he would be closely matched with See More Business; good chance.

VERDICT With likely front-runner **Beau**, overrated and with improvement to find, taking them along this will hopefully be run at a true gallop. **See More Business** would just about be the one to beat if back in top form but he is 11 now and did disappoint last time. Preference has to be for **CYFOR MALTA**, with his absence since winning this two years ago most unlikely to be a drawback. His form back then suggests he will be a tough opponent at these weights even for a peak-form See More Buisness. [MCu]

POSTDATA Beau | TOPSPEED Beau

attributed to *Post* writer Mel Cullinan) and selections from two of the paper's other columns, Postdata and Topspeed.

Postdata and Topspeed both plumped for Beau; Spotlight selected Cyfor Malta; and Postmark has See More Business top rated. Postmark was right: See More Business won.

The form of See More Business in the *Racing Post* on the morning of the Pillar Property Chase at Cheltenham on 27 January 2001.

See More Business is carrying eleven stone ten pounds in the race. He is an eleven-year-old bay gelding by the stallion Seymour Hicks out of the mare Miss Redlands, who herself is by Dubassoff. He is trained by P. F. Nicholls and will be ridden by M. A. Fitzgerald.

There follows a summary of his placings in his last seventeen outings ('C' indicates 'carried out'). The official rating of See More Business is 174. He has run in twenty-one steeplechases, twenty-four jumps races in all, and his placings and win and place prize money are stated. Then comes a list of all his wins, in reverse order beginning with the most recent, at Wetherby in October 2000 – a Class A, Grade 2 steeplechase over three miles one furlong in soft going which brought his owners £27,000. At the foot of that list comes his total win prize money (£493,938). Of his outings on today's going – soft – he has won four and not been placed from six outings; the same breakdown is given for today's course (two wins, no places from five outings) and distance (four, zero, five).

His last outing was at Kempton Park on 26 December 2000, when he was fifth. For his form, you need to consult the entry on Beau, who is running in this race and finished in front of See More Business that day.

The outing before that had been at Wetherby on 28 October 2000: that Class A Grade Two steeplechase worth £27,000 to the winner. Four ran, the going was soft, there were eighteen fences in the race, the time of the race was 6 minutes 34.1 seconds, which was thirteen seconds slower than standard for that distance at that course.

See More Business was then ten, carried eleven stone twelve pounds, wore blinkers, was ridden by M. A. Fitzgerald and started 3-1 on favourite. Then follows a summary of how he ran his race, a note of his ratings that day by Postmark and Topspeed and his official rating, a note of fluctuations in his price (touched 11-4 on and 7-2 on). Bobby Grant (aged nine, carrying eleven stone twelve pounds, ridden by A. Dobbin, started 9-1) was second and Young Kenny third. The distances were thirty lengths, twelve lengths and half a length. The new Postmark ratings for the first three are 188+, 164+ and 132+ (the plus sign indicating further improvement to come). The Racecheck feature summarises subsequent outings of horses who ran in that race, as a simple way of establishing the quality of the form: between them the runners have won two races (of which one was in the same class of race as today), been placed in none and unplaced in five.

See More Business 11-10

11-y-o *b g Seymour Hicks - Miss Redlands (Dubassoff)*

P F Nicholls M A FitzGerald

Placings: 3111C/41P31/11141-15

OR174	Starts	1st	2nd	3rd	Win & Pl
Chase	21	11	2	2	£514,603
All Jumps races	24	14	2	2	£530,730

	10/00	**Weth**	3m1f A Gd2 Ch soft	£27,000
	4/00	**Aint**	3m1f A Gd2 Ch good	£46,900
	2/00	**Newb**	3m B Ch gd-sft	£31,000
	12/99	**Kemp**	3m A Gd1 Ch soft	£65,500
	10/99	**Weth**	3m1f A Gd2 Ch good	£23,800
	3/99	**Chel**	3m2½f A Gd1 Ch gd-sft	£149,600
172	**12/98**	**Chep**	3m A Gd2 Ch Hcap good	£20,306
	1/98	**Chel**	3m1½f B Ch gd-sft	£16,938
	12/97	**Kemp**	3m A Gd1 Ch soft	£64,375
157	**12/97**	**Chep**	3m A Gd2 Ch Hcap soft	£18,606
	11/96	**Chep**	2m3½f A Nov Gd2 Ch gd-sft	£13,786
	12/95	**Sand**	2m6f A Nov Gd2 Hdl good	£9,555
	11/95	**Winc**	2m6f C Nov Hdl good	£3,727
	11/95	**Chep**	2m4½f D Nov Hdl gd-sft	£2,845

Total win prize-money £493,938

Going (S): 4-0-6 **Course:** 2-0-5 **Distance:** 4-0-5

26 Dec 00 Kempton 5th, see **BEAU**

28 Oct 00 Wetherby 3m1f A Gd2 Ch £27,000
4 ran SOFT 18fncs Time 6m 34.10s (slw 13.00s)
1 **SEE MORE BUSINESS** 10 11-12 b ....M A FitzGerald 1/3F
close up, led 6th, clear from halfway, jumped badly left and blundered 3 out, went left last, unchallenged
[PM188 TS180 OR174] [tchd 4/11 & 2/7]
2 Bobby Grant 9 11-12 ....A Dobbin 9/1
3 Young Kenny 9 11-6 ....R Garritty 9/1
Dist: 30-12-½ RACE PM: 188+/164+/132+
Racecheck: Wins 2 (1) Pl - Unpl 5

6 Apr 00 Aintree 3m1f A Gd2 Ch £46,900
4 ran GOOD 19fncs Time 6m 29.20s (slw 2.70s)
1 **SEE MORE BUSINESS** 10 12-0 b ....M A FitzGerald 5/4F
made all, mistake 4th, blundered 12th, joined 13th, left well clear 14th, mistake 4 out, not extended
[PM188 TS139 OR175] [op 11/8 tchd 6/4]
2 Mulligan 10 11-4 ....A Maguire 7/1
3 Lake Kariba 9 11-4 ....A P McCoy 5/1
Dist: 21-dist RACE PM: 188+/147
Racecheck: Wins 1 (1) Pl 1 Unpl 2

16 Mar 00 Cheltenham 3m2½f A Gd1 Ch £162,400
12 ran GD-FM 22fncs Time 6m 30.30s (fst 17.30s)
1 Looks Like Trouble 8 12-0 ....R Johnson 9/2
2 Florida Pearl 8 12-0 ....P Carberry 9/2
3 Strong Promise 9 12-0 ....R Thornton 20/1
4 **SEE MORE BUSINESS** 10 12-0 b ....M A FitzGerald 9/4F
tracked leader from 3rd until led 11th, headed 13th, stayed 2nd to 17th, lost place under pressure after 3 out, rallied and stayed on again run-in [PM176 TS145 OR177] [op 2/1 tchd 5/2]
Dist: 5-nk-¾-nk-dist RACE PM: 183+/178+/176
Racecheck: Wins 4 (2) Pl 1 Unpl 10

12 Feb 00 Newbury 3m B Ch £31,000
6 ran GD-SFT 18fncs Time 6m 22.10s (slw 19.00s)
1 **SEE MORE BUSINESS** 10 11-10 b ....M A FitzGerald 1/3F
tracked leader from 2nd until led 8th, not fluent 11th to 13th, hit 4 out, came clear from next, very easily
[PM188 TS140 OR177] [op 2/7 tchd 4/11]
2 Macgeorge 10 11-10 ....N Williamson 25/1
3 Tresor de Mai 6 11-4 b ....A P McCoy 15/2
Dist: 18-nk-dist RACE PM: 188+/159+/155+
Racecheck: Wins 1 (1) Pl - Unpl 8

27 Dec 99 Kempton 3m A Gd1 Ch £65,500
9 ran SOFT 19fncs Time 6m 8.10s (slw 0.70s)
1 **SEE MORE BUSINESS** 9 11-10 b ....M A FitzGerald 5/2F
always leading trio, pressed leader from 10th until led after 4 out, soon well clear, impressive
[PM188 TS161 OR170] [op 9/4 tchd 11/4]
2 Go Ballistic 10 11-10 ....R Johnson 7/1
3 Dr Leunt 8 11-10 ....A Thornton 13/2
Dist: 17-19-19-27 RACE PM: 188+/170+/149+
Racecheck: Wins 3 (2) Pl 3 Unpl 11

30 Jan 99 Cheltenham 3rd, see **CYFOR MALTA**

Comparisons are not necessarily odious . . .

TRAINER FORM	GOING HY	DIST 33.0l	COURSE	ABILITY	RECENT FORM	GROUP ENTRY	3.50	Topspeed Ratings LATEST	BEST	ADJUSTED
✓	✓✓	✓	?	✓✓	✓	G3	Edmond	123	132-Dec 02 Chep 24.0hy	132
✓	✓	?	?	✓✓	✓✓	G3	Murt's Man	144	144-Jan 25 Winc 25.5s	144
✓	✓✓	?	?	✓✓	✓✓		Narrow Water	104	130-Dec 02 Weth 20.5s	130
✓	✓	✓	✓	✓✓	✓		b1 Seven Towers	129	129-Jan 13 Newc 30.0s	129
✗	✓✓	✓	?	✓	✓	G3	Him Of Praise	142	142-Feb 03 Uttx 28.0hy	142
✓	✓✓	?	?	✓✓	✗	G3	Lady Of Gortmerron	-	136-Nov 25 Hayd 28.5hy	136
✓	✓✓	?	?	✓	✗		b1 Campaign	114	134-Mar 11 Ayr 25.0hy	134
✗	✓✓	✓	?	✓✓	✓	G3	Royal Tommy	135	135-Feb 09 Bang 30.0hy	135
✓✓	✓✓	✓	✓	✓✓✓	✓✓	G3	Scotton Green	**154**	**155**-Nov 12 Weth 25.0hy	**155**
✓	✓✓	✓	?	?	?		Saxon Duke	-		
✗	✓	✓	✓	✓✓✓	✗		Mister Muddypaws	125	149-May 05 Sedg 28.0gf	149
✓✓	✓	✓	?	✓	✓	G3	Riot Leader	-	50-Dec 26 MRas 33.0s	50

POSTDATA Scotton Green **TOPSPEED** Scotton Green

The *Racing Post*'s Postdata and Topspeed chart for the Tote Northern National at Newcastle on 17 February 2001 weighs such factors as the current form of the trainer, the suitability of the going and course, proven ability of the horse, most recent form and whether they have entries in top races in the future. The Topspeed column provides a comparative chart of the horse's latest rating and its best, adjusted to today's weights.

OFFICIAL RATINGS LAST SIX OUTINGS-LATEST ON RIGHT						3.50 HANDICAP		TODAY	FUTURE	POSTMARK LATEST	BEST	ADJUSTED
126^1	136^2	140^P	137^9	134^3	134^3	Edmond	11-10	130		135	149	156 ◄
—	—	110^2	115^F	115^2	115^1	Murt's Man	11-5	125		154 ◄	154	154
—	—	—	—	—	—	Narrow Water	11-5	125		149	149	156 ◄
145^U	—	135^5	130^4	121^5	116^1	Seven Towers	11-2	122		147	147	149
140^3	140^5	139^2	130^7	126^8	122^4	Him Of Praise	11-0	120		132	135	148
—	100^1	107^2	110^2	110^1	116^U	Lady Of Gortmerron	10-10	116		—	158 ◄	155
—	—	—	128^P	—	120^4	Campaign	10-9	115		120	148	148
104^1	129^P	117^1	121^8	122^7	118^3	Royal Tommy	10-9	115		126	154	154
129^7	119^2	119^F	116^P	114^5	110^2	Scotton Green	10-4	110		150	156	156 ◄
103^1	108^3	107^2	112^3	113^4	111^8	Saxon Duke	10-3	109		—	—	154
108^P	104^1	109^P	107^1	112^7	110^5	Mister Muddypaws	10-3	109		127	156	151
78^1	82^1	—	111^P	104^2	116^P	Riot Leader	9-12	106	-2	—	—	—

Another comparative chart: the Postmark ratings for the Tote Northern National, showing each runner's official rating on its last six outings and its latest and best Postmark figure adjusted to that day's weights. The three horses joint top-rated by Postmark included the 6–1 winner, Narrow Water.

Regular practice at studying comparative charts like these soon cuts a great deal of the drudgery out of form study.

Whatever you want to know about a horse's form, it's somewhere in the *Racing Post*. The trouble is, in many cases the more you know, the more confused and indecisive you become.

The official form book record of the Pillar Property Chase at Cheltenham on 27 January 2001.

The description is headed by the Raceform reference number of that race (3321) followed by race name, grade, age range and class. The race was due to start at 2.50 and actually went off at 2.55, over three miles one and a half furlongs, taking in twenty-one fences. Then are given the amounts of prize money won by first, second and third. Observant readers will note that See More Business's owners netted £49,125, rather than the £45,000 that morning's *Racing Post* declared to be the winning prize money (see page 56). Why the change? Look at what happened to Lord Noelie . . .

'GOING plus 0.8 per fur (S)' indicates that the going was soft and that the Raceform Going Allowance for that race was 0.8 seconds per furlong – that is, the state of the going meant that the winner could be expected to take 0.8 seconds per furlong more than standard time for that distance.

The winner See More Business has last run in race 2709 (the Pertemps King George VI Chase at Kempton Park) and finished fifth. It was thirty-two days since that run, and for this race he is officially rated 174. He is trained by P. F. Nicholls, is an eleven-year-old who carried eleven stone ten pounds and wore blinkers, and was ridden by M. A. Fitzgerald. Then comes, in parentheses, a bare description of his running in the Pillar Property Chase, expressed in the clipped shorthand of the form book which in this case translates to: 'led the field; made a mistake at the sixth fence; went clear from the tenth; blundered four out; soon recovered; came clear from three out; was not challenged'. His starting price was 9-4 second favourite; his Raceform Rating is 176+; and his speed figure relates to a complicated timing formula which can be used when assessing future races.

Beau had also last run in race 2709, while Cyfor Malta (who started 13-8 favourite) had not had a previous race that season. The betting percentages added up to 104.6, making the book on this race 4.6 over-round (see pages 77–8).

The time of the race was 6 minutes, 59.9 seconds, 12.7 seconds slower than standard time.

The Computer Straight Forecast paid £7.28. The Tote paid a dividend of £2.70 for the win and £6.50 for the Exacta predicting first and second. (There was no other Tote betting on this four-runner race.) The owners were Paul

3321 PILLAR PROPERTY CHASE GRADE 2 (6-Y-O+) (Class A)
2:50 (2:55) **3m 1½f (21 fncs)** £49,125.00 (£17,250.00; £8,625.00) GOING plus 0.8 per fur (S)

			SP	RR	SF
2709^{5}	**See More Business (IRE)** ^{32} **(174)** (PFNicholls) **11-11-10b** MAFitzgerald (led: mstke 6th: clr 10th: blnd 4 out: sn rcvrd: c clr fr 3 out: unchal) ....---	1	$9/4^{2}$	176+	114
2709^{4}	**Beau (IRE)** ^{32} **(154)** (NATwiston-Davies) **8-11-6** CLlewellyn (chsd wnr most of way: rdn and no imp fr 4 out) dist	2	$11/4^{3}$	---	---
	Cyfor Malta (FR) ^{728} (MCPipe) **8-11-0** APMcCoy (hld up in rr: nt fluent: lft 3rd 7th: hdwy to dispute 2nd 4 out: wknd rpdly nxt: t.o) ....dist	3	$13/8^{1}$	---	---
1660^{4}	**Lord Noelie (IRE)** ^{97} **(149)** (MissHCKnight) **8-11-5** JCulloty (disp 2nd tl blnd and uns rdr 7th) ....---	U	10/1	---	---

(SP 104.6%) **4 Rn**

6m 59.90s (12.70) CSF £7.28 TOTE £2.70 ; EX £6.50 OWNER Paul K Barber & Robert Ogden (DITCHEAT, SOMERSET) BRED Ian Bryant

2709 See More Business (IRE) put himself firmly back in the Gold Cup picture on this softer ground, which is the key to him. However, the fact he made two bad mistakes is a worry, and it seems the effect the blinkers have had on his jumping may be wearing off. (9/4)

2709 Beau (IRE) , two lengths in front of a lacklustre See More Business in the King George, was put firmly in his place. He is yet to prove he is nothing more than a good handicapper. (11/4)

Cyfor Malta (FR) , having his first outing since winning this race two years ago, was short of peak fitness. It is going to take tremendous improvement in six weeks to enable him to win the Gold Cup. (13/8F)

K. Barber and Robert Ogden; the horse was trained at Ditcheat, Somerset, and bred by Ian Bryant. The notebook comments at the foot of the entry add to the clipped account of how each horse ran the race and look at the wider picture – for instance, whether the effect of blinkers on See More Business's jumping is wearing off, or whether Cyfor Malta has a real chance in the Gold Cup.

Big Mac's exclusive guide to the betting jungle

John McCririck

So Jimbo has put you straight on all the mysteries of form and what to do with it. You've studied the race, scrutinised the runners in the paddock, and made your selection. Now it's time to put your money where your mouth is – and bet!

Come with me into the steaming jungle of the betting ring, that bubbling cauldron of activity where every day hundreds of thousands of pounds are won and lost. Here's where you are buffeted by punters desperate to get the 'ear 'ole' (6–4) while it lasts, where you pick up, or 'earwig', last-minute gossip and rumours, where wads of money go into – and sometimes out of – bookies' satchels.

It's noisy, it's frenetic, it can be manic – and there's nowhere like it on earth.

Not everybody is able to join in the cut and thrust of the racecourse ring: 95 per cent of wagering on horses in Britain takes place in betting shops or on credit, and some of you have the luxury of striking your bet over the phone or even on the internet as you watch Channel Four Racing – though turn the sound down when that burbling, arm-waving fatso in the betting ring comes on!

However you bet, contemplate my golden rules – without, please, pausing to wonder whether I've always kept to them myself. If I have, why am I, a failed 'investor' and bookmaker, still scratching a meagre living with Channel Four? . . .

Bet within your means

The most obvious advice, but one which some people sadly ignore: never, ever, bet more than you can afford to lose. Decide in advance your limit, and don't exceed it – however tempting that bet in the desperate Getting Out Stakes. Always remember there's another day. It's a perfectly natural desire to be 'in front' and leave course or betting shop with that glow of satisfaction – and bulging pockets – but never chase your losses. So simple to write!

Be disciplined

Unlike bookmakers, you don't have to bet on every race. The exercise of patience, waiting for the right betting opportunity, is a vital weapon in any good punter's artillery, and all the professional punters – yes, there are some who really do make a living from the game – are celebrated for their patience. Exercise restraint, and you'll do much better in the long term.

Come racing!

Never mind lying in your pit at home watching those know-alls on Channel Four. Come racing, where there are crucial betting advantages.

At last, the betting jungle is becoming customer-friendly, caring, like all progressive businesses.

Look what you get:

- No betting tax – you'll be paying 9 per cent off-course – until Gordon Brown's hugely welcome abolition of betting duty takes effect.
- The chance to bet at the very last minute, when you've been able to study the runners at close quarters in the paddock, watch them go down to the start, absorb all the clues and pick up racecourse gossip.
- The opportunity to shop around for the best prices in the betting ring.
- Betting without the favourite, in running, on stewards' enquiries and so on.
- The chance (not available in a shop) to 'take the fractions' and bet £25 to £4, rather than 6–1, or 100–6 rather than 16–1. Most course bookmakers will offer the 'fracs' – and if one won't, just go elsewhere.

I've said it before and I'll say it again:
Come racing!

Keep records

Systematic recording of all your bets reveals patterns and preferences from which you can benefit, and the effort of disciplined record-keeping will be well rewarded. At the very least record:

- date
- stake
- type of bet – and whether placed well in advance of race or just before
- selection(s)
- odds – and whether this was a board price, SP, ante-post, etc.
- type of race
- result
- running balance of year's betting (which can be very instructive!)

Periodically study your records for valuable insights into your punting strengths and weaknesses. What you discover will be potentially profitable in the future. It could be to avoid handicaps, or betting odds-on. Sometimes the trends revealed can be alarming. Learn from them.

To encourage you in this most crucial of punting habits, we've printed at the back of this book a grid where you can record your own bets. Be honest when you fill it in, now!

Shop around – and don't ignore the Tote

Never rush in to take the first price you see. In the morning, weigh up the range of prices published in the press. On course, take a look at all prices available in the ring. Work out the value price you reckon your fancy should be offered at. Resolve never to take less. With sound judgement of odds the winners missed will be more than made up for by avoiding taking a chance with those underpriced.

And when shopping around remember Alastair Down's tip at the front of this book: *always check the Tote.*

Although the Tote is sometimes thought of as a medium for small punters rather than the big hitters, it's invariably worth keeping an eye on the Tote screens if you've come racing – and especially if you're interested in an outsider. The watchword always is to compare the prices: had you been perspicacious enough to choose Jet Ski Lady for the eight-runner 1991 Oaks and back her on the Tote, you'd not have been best pleased with the return of £16.50 – equivalent to 15½–1. Her returned starting price was 50–1. But when Jenny Pitman sent out Royal Athlete to land The Cuddly One her second Grand National in 1994, Tote backers had a return of £83.70 to a £1 stake, while backers at SP were rewarded with a comparatively measly 40–1, less than half the Tote odds.

You can't be definitive about when to back on the Tote, though as a rule Tote prices tend to be skinnier than the bookies' about an obviously popular runner – one owned by the Queen, for instance, or a horse who has captured the imagination like the greys Desert Orchid or the ill-fated One Man. Horses with sexy names, like Good In Bed or Virile Mac, or those ridden by star jockeys such as Frankie Dettori and Tony McCoy, attract the small-time punters, and they tend to favour the Tote's wonderful Ladies in Red over those fierce, intimidating bookmakers in the betting ring! That's one reason why the whole ethos of the jungle is being radically revised as racing reaches the new millennium, with the aim of making the arena far more consumer-friendly.

Study the statistics

When that moron on Channel Four Racing starts banging on about 'only four winning favourites in thirty-one runnings of this race', don't switch over. The statistical profile of some races can be extremely significant, and it's yet another factor to bear in mind when making a bet. Of the last thirty-eight runnings of the Derby, twenty-five have gone to the first or second favourite. Of the last forty-four runnings of the Ayr Gold Cup, just three have been won by the favourite. In which race would you be more comfortable backing a market leader?

Back to basics!

Punters who do not understand the basic principles of betting are putting themselves at a hopeless disadvantage in the perpetual battle against the bookies. You don't need a master's degree in maths – I couldn't even pass my Elementary Maths O-Level – but get a grasp of the bare essentials and in the long run your betting will be much more efficient – and profitable.

Stick to those few gems of good sense and you'll be well equipped to hold your own in the tantalising, exhilarating but so often frustrating world of wagering.

Good luck!

The betting business

Sean Magee

BETTING BASICS

A punter wanting to bet on a horse has a choice:

- to bet with a bookmaker, who prices up the race on the basis of his assessment of the chances of each horse and then alters those odds according to the flow of money on each particular runner;
- to bet with the Tote, a pool system where the backers all put their money in and the winners share the payout;
- to bet 'on the spread', where you can 'buy' or 'sell' on your opinion regarding whether the firm's view of an outcome is too high or too low (see pages 110–14).

Bookmakers' odds lengthen (offering a higher return) or shorten (offering a lower one) according to how money is being wagered, but the odds at which you strike your bet remain valid for that transaction whatever happens subsequently, unless you bet at starting price – the odds at which the horse is officially declared to have started the race.

On the Tote, you will not know the exact return on your stake until after the race.

Odds

Occasionally people are perplexed by what commonly expressed odds – 6–5, say, or 13–8 – actually mean. This list gives a few of the odds frequently quoted in horse racing expressed in more familiar fractions:

Evens	1 to 1
11–10	$1\frac{1}{10}$ to 1
6–5	$1\frac{1}{5}$ to 1
5–4	$1\frac{1}{4}$ to 1
11–8	$1\frac{3}{8}$ to 1
6–4	$1\frac{1}{2}$ to 1
13–8	$1\frac{5}{8}$ to 1
7–4	$1\frac{3}{4}$ to 1
15–8	$1\frac{7}{8}$ to 1
85–40	$2\frac{1}{8}$ to 1
9–4	$2\frac{1}{4}$ to 1
5–2	$2\frac{1}{2}$ to 1
11–4	$2\frac{3}{4}$ to 1
100–30	$3\frac{1}{3}$ to 1
7–2	$3\frac{1}{2}$ to 1
9–2	$4\frac{1}{2}$ to 1
11–2	$5\frac{1}{2}$ to 1
13–2	$6\frac{1}{2}$ to 1
15–2	$7\frac{1}{2}$ to 1
17–2	$8\frac{1}{2}$ to 1

Spread betting can involve huge gains, or losses, though back-up positions can usually be taken as the bet unfolds.

Odds

Odds are simply an expression of probability: a way of representing the likelihood, as perceived by the person laying the odds, of the horse winning or losing. (We'll come on to each-way betting later.)

So, a bookie who quotes a particular horse at evens (1–1) thinks that there is an equal (50 per cent) chance of the horse winning and losing. At 2–1 against there is a 33.33 per cent chance of its winning and a 66.67 per cent chance of its losing: that is, two out of every three chances – 2 plus 1 equals 3 – are against its winning. At 2–1 on (the 'on' indicating that the odds are reversed, '2–1 on' being the common way of expressing 1–2) there is a 66.67 per cent chance of its winning and a 33.33 per cent chance of its losing. So any horse at 'odds on' is deemed more likely to win than lose. (A useful way of thinking about odds is that, with odds against, the first number expressed is the multiple of your stake that you will win, the second number the amount that the bookie will keep if you lose – or, if you like, your stake unit. Thus at 6–1 against you put down one to win six.)

Note that these are judgements of the perceived likelihood of a particular outcome – perceived, that is, by the bookmaker. The canny way to approach betting is to weigh up your own opinion of the horse's chance of winning against the bookmaker's, and to back your fancy if the odds on offer are longer than you feel represent that chance: such a bet represents 'value', the 'bargain' which every regular punter seeks.

Cue John McCririck: 'Judge all the factors involved. Then assess, objectively, the likely probability of any horse winning. If the odds on offer are far bigger, check for any late developments – sweating or unruly behaviour in the paddock, going down to post badly or negatives in the betting ring.

'If you still believe the price is tempting, step in. If not, keep out!'

Odds percentages

Odds on	*Price*	*Odds against*
50.00	Evens	50.00
52.38	11–10	47.62
54.55	6–5	45.45
55.56	5–4	44.44
57.89	11–8	42.11
60.00	6–4	40.00
61.90	13–8	38.10
63.64	7–4	36.36
65.22	15–8	34.78
66.67	2–1	33.33
68.00	85–40	32.00
69.23	9–4	30.77
71.43	5–2	28.57
73.33	11–4	26.67
75.00	3–1	25.00
76.92	100–30	23.08
77.78	7–2	22.22
80.00	4–1	20.00
81.82	9–2	18.18

Odds percentages (continued)

Odds on	*Price*	*Odds against*
83.33	5–1	16.67
84.62	11–2	15.38
85.71	6–1	14.29
86.67	13–2	13.33
87.50	7–1	12.50
88.24	15–2	11.76
88.89	8–1	11.11
89.47	17–2	10.53
90.00	9–1	10.00
90.91	10–1	9.09
91.67	11–1	8.33
92.31	12–1	7.69
92.86	13–1	7.14
93.33	14–1	6.67
93.75	15–1	6.25
94.12	16–1	5.88
95.24	20–1	4.76
95.65	22–1	4.35
96.15	25–1	3.85
97.06	33–1	2.94
97.56	40–1	2.44
98.04	50–1	1.96
98.51	66–1	1.49
98.77	80–1	1.23
99.01	100–1	0.99
99.60	250–1	0.40
99.80	500–1	0.20

Betting with a bookmaker

A lot of people find the mysteries of betting with a bookmaker – the maths, the jargon, the ritual, to say nothing of the associated arm-waving of men in white gloves – completely impenetrable. And yet the majority of the population have a bet with a bookie at least once a year, even if it is just £1 each way on the Grand National, on which over £80 million was supposedly staked in 2000.

In fact, the principle of betting with a bookmaker is simple: he offers odds at which you may pitch your money against his. The practice and the maths, however, can be less clear. Nor is confusion restricted to the arcane refinements of multiple wagers: one of the most widespread mistakes about betting is that once you've handed your stake over to the bookie that's the last you see of it – even if your horse wins and you get a handsome return. But if that were the case, why would anyone ever bet at odds on?

If your betting is to be effective, you need to know not only how to do it yourself, but how the betting market works, and that means understanding the mathematical factors that govern it. You may think this doesn't matter; but the bookmakers know it does, and unless you have the rudiments of how a book is constructed you'll be putting yourself at a disadvantage to start with. Conversely, a punter who knows how a book works and what factors affect the prices is a punter well poised to take advantage of market moves.

The over-round book

Face facts. The average punter cannot win, for it is the

bookmaker who constructs the odds (the 'book') for each race – and he does so in such a way that, in the long term, he will make a profit. How?

Mathematically, if the probabilities of winning of all the horses in a particular race are added up, they must total exactly 100 per cent. What the bookmaker does to guarantee his profitability is ensure that the total of the percentage probabilities he quotes – the odds he offers – for each race exceeds 100 per cent.

As an example, we can look at the returned starting prices for the Pertemps King George VI Chase at Kempton Park on Boxing Day 2000:

horse	*SP*	%
See More Business	6–4	40.00
First Gold	5–2	28.57
Florida Pearl	11–2	15.38
Edredon Bleu	9–1	10.00
Beau	14–1	6.67
Go Ballistic	14–1	6.67
Lady Cricket	16–1	5.88
Bellator	33–1	2.94
Double Thriller	66–1	1.49
total percentages		117.60

In strictly mathematical terms, the total of those percentages should be 100 – yet the actual total is over 117. That difference represents the layers' theoretical profit.

A book in which the probabilities add up to over 100 per cent is described as 'over-round', and in this case the book is over-round by 17.6 per cent, which means that for every £117.60 the bookmaker takes in bets, he theoretically expects to have to pay out £100, leaving him £17.60 profit. When a book is over-round the punter cannot back every runner and be guaranteed a return, and as every efficient bookmaker will be betting over-round this quickly disposes of the notion that you can guarantee to win by backing every horse in a race.

Bookmakers do not, of course, take money evenly across the whole field, nor do they win on every race; but by maintaining the over-roundness of the book they are ensuring that in the long term they will have to pay out less than they take in. (A set of odds in which the aggregate percentages total under 100 is described as 'over-broke'.)

Comparing the odds

Comparing the odds offered by different bookmakers is the key to finding the best value in a race. Every day the *Racing Post* publishes the Pricewise column with a chart comparing the early prices on that day's major events, as well as regular ante-post updates. Very occasionally these will indicate ways in which, by shopping around and backing different runners with different bookmakers – usually in small fields – you can find an 'over-broke' book and guarantee yourself a win.

Several national newspapers now provide a similar service.

Constructing the book

For the really big races the betting will begin a long way in advance of the event – weeks, even months, occasionally years in advance. For other key races the major bookmakers advertise prices on the morning of the race, and punters may back at these prices – which may go up and down according to the amounts of money being wagered – until the proper book is formed before the race itself. (A 'steamer' is a horse which has been heavily backed off-course before the actual pre-race market has been formed.)

Books tend to be more over-round in competitive handicaps: the book for the Tote Cambridgeshire at Newmarket on 30 September 2000, won by Katy Nowaitee, was over-round by 50.2 per cent.

The bookmakers employ form and betting experts to draw up the 'tissue', a forecast of how the betting on the race will open on the course, and the course bookmakers (whose activities dictate the officially returned starting price) will probably start out betting to these prices, adjusting them subsequently according to the general response to the prices and to their own judgement of the probable outcome of the race. The more punters back the winner, and the longer the odds at which they do so, the more the bookie is going to have to pay out; so if he takes a lot of money on one horse he will shorten its price in order to dissuade other punters from backing it, while if (for whatever reason) he thinks that a horse will not win, or he can't lay it, he will lengthen its price in order to tempt punters who think they know better than he does.

While all this is going on – bets being made, prices adjusted, judgements formed – the bookmaker will be constantly aware of his own liabilities, and if what he stands to have to pay out on one horse is more than he can comfortably cover from losing bets on the other runners he may decide to 'lay off' – that is, to pass all or some of the money he has taken on that horse on to other bookmakers – in other words, betting on that horse himself. It is these transactions, the bets made by course bookies among themselves, that are communicated by the sign language of 'tic-tac'.

> The race with the most open betting ever was the 1964 Grand National, when Flying Wild, Laffy, Pappageno's Cottage and Time were co-favourites at 100–7.

The biggest movements of money, however, are not among the course bookies, but between the off-course bookmakers and their counterparts at the track: for some of the money wagered away from the course, in betting shops and through credit accounts with the big bookmakers, can be brought into the ring in order that the returned starting prices – which are determined by the on-course market – accurately reflect the weight of money wagered on the race. This is done through representatives of the off-course bookmakers, some of whom will bet at the track to put their off-course money into the market. The 'magic sign' is the tic-tac signal (somewhat like drawing a halo over the head) which indicates money from Ladbrokes – the largest bookmaker in Britain – being brought into the market.

TYPES OF BET

There are many different types of bet, some of them involving procedures and permutations of brain-aching complexity. Combination bets, despite the demands they make on the mental powers of the backer, and despite the fact that they are difficult to pull off, are attractive to small punters as they offer the promise of big returns for modest outlay.

The most usual types of bet, and some of the more exotic, are described briefly here, with sample calculations which exclude any allowance for tax.

Win

You bet on the horse to come first. The tax-free return on a £5 win bet at 6–1 is £35: £5 stake plus £30 winnings.

Each way

You bet on the horse either to win or to be placed – that is

- to finish in the first two in races of five, six or seven runners
- to finish in the first three in races of eight or more runners
- or to finish in the first four in handicaps with sixteen or more runners.

These stipulations can vary from one bookmaker to another, and some pay out on the fifth place in very competitive big races. Shop around for the best terms.

The odds for a place are normally one-quarter or one-fifth the odds for a win, depending on the nature of the race and the number of runners: the bookmaker will advertise the fraction.

An each-way bet is in fact two bets – one for the win and one for the place – and consequently the stake will be twice the unit of the bet: thus a bet of £5 each way costs £10. A bet of £5 each way (with the place odds one-quarter the win odds) on a horse which wins at 10–1 returns winnings of £62.50 (£50 win plus £12.50 place, as the winning horse is also placed) plus your stake of £10 – a total return (tax-free) of £72.50. If the horse is second you win £12.50 and have your stake on the place bet returned, but lose your £5 win bet: so your return on the £10 invested is £17.50. Obviously it is not worth backing a horse each way if its odds are much less than 5–1, as the amount you will make on the place bet if it is placed but does not win will not cover your loss on the win bet: the calculations for off-course bets are further complicated by the need to allow for tax, but it should be clear that an on-course each-way bet at 4–1, one-quarter the odds a place, will yield no gain and no loss if the horse is placed but does not win.

Place

Not many bookmakers will bet for place only, though the Tote runs a Place pool on every race with five or more runners (see page 93).

Combination bets

These are individual bets which combine two or more horses in a single wager: if one horse loses the whole bet is lost. (Note: if your selection is a non-runner, the number of elements of the combination bet reduces accordingly – treble becomes double, double becomes single – and stakes are apportioned *pro rata*.) The permutations are infinite, but the most common versions include the following.

Double

You bet on two horses in different races. If the first wins, the return – winnings and stake – go on to the second.

A simple way of calculating the winnings on a double is to add one to each of the odds, multiply them, subtract one from the total and multiply by the stake. A £5 double on horses which both win at 2–1 is an 8–1 double, yielding a return of £45 – £40 winnings plus £5 stake – as the first win gives a return of £15, which then goes on the second horse at 2–1 and brings £30 winnings plus £15 stake: £45.

You will not get a bookmaker to accept a double bet calculated in this way on two events where the first result has a direct bearing on the second. Had you wanted to back Nayef to win both the Two Thousand Guineas and Derby in 2001, the odds quoted would have been shorter than a simple multiple of the single odds for both eventualities, as success in the first would significantly increase the chances of success in the second.

Treble

You bet on three horses in different races. Again, add one to each of the winning odds, multiply them, and subtract one from the total to find the winnings. So a £5 treble on three horses which each win at 2–1 yields a return of £135: winnings of £130 plus the £5 stake.

Accumulator

On the same principle, you bet on any number of horses to win different races, calculating the winnings in the same way as for a double or a treble. The old ITV Seven was a seven-horse accumulator: had your seven choices in a £5 accumulator all obliged at 2–1 you would have relieved your bookmaker of £10,930 in winnings.

Multiple bets

These are ways of combining different bets on several horses in various ways. Unlike combination bets, success does not depend on each horse winning: the names under which such bets go are simply a shorthand for a recognized menu of individual bets. Multiple bets can be win or each way.

Patent

Combines three different horses in different races in seven separate bets – three singles, three doubles, and one treble.

Thus if the three horses selected are Angelic, Buttercup and Cowpat, the Patent consists of:

3 singles on: Angelic
Buttercup
Cowpat
3 doubles: Angelic with Buttercup
Angelic with Cowpat

Buttercup with Cowpat
1 treble: Angelic with Buttercup with Cowpat

A £1 win Patent will cost you £7; a £1 each-way Patent costs £14. Say you have a £1 win Patent on Angelic, Buttercup and Cowpat and they all win at 2–1; your winnings are:

£6 (three £1 singles each winning at 2–1); plus
£24 (three £1 doubles with each horse winning at 2–1); plus
£26 (a £1 treble with each horse winning at 2–1), producing a total of £56.

If two of the horses win at 2–1 while the third loses, you would still make a profit. You win £4 (two £1 singles each winning at 2–1) plus £8 (one £1 double with each horse winning at 2–1): total winnings £12. But of your seven bets four (one single, two doubles, one treble) have lost, so your profit is £12 less £4: £8.

Trixie

A Patent without the singles: three horses combined in three doubles and one treble (four bets).

Yankee

Combines four different horses in different races in eleven bets (so a £1 win Yankee costs £11). The horses are connected in

- six doubles
- four trebles
- one four-horse accumulator.

Have a Yankee on the three horses we've just backed in a Patent and a fourth, Dunderhead. The bet looks like this:

6 doubles	Angelic and Buttercup
	Angelic and Cowpat
	Angelic and Dunderhead
	Buttercup and Cowpat
	Buttercup and Dunderhead
	Cowpat and Dunderhead
4 trebles	Angelic, Buttercup, Cowpat
	Angelic, Cowpat, Dunderhead
	Angelic, Buttercup, Dunderhead
	Buttercup, Cowpat, Dunderhead
1 accumulator	Angelic, Buttercup, Cowpat, Dunderhead

Should all four win at 2–1, our £1 win Yankee wins . . . no, work it out for yourself!

Lucky 15

A fifteen-bet wager adding four singles to the eleven bets of the Yankee. If one selection wins but the other four lose, many bookmakers will benevolently double the odds for your single winning bet, and there is usually a bonus for picking all four winners.

Super Yankee

Also known as a Canadian. Combines five selections in

- ten doubles
- ten trebles

- five four-horse accumulators
- one five-horse accumulator

– a total of twenty-six bets.

> The bookies may consider accumulators 'mugs' bets', but in May 1995 a lady pensioner in Nottingham begged to differ. She staked a five pence accumulator on five horses, and for good measure added a Super Flag (a multiple bet of baffling complexity) on the same quintet. The result . . .
>
> - Christian Flight won at 20–1
> - Don't Forget Ruby won at 12–1
> - Romany Creek won at 20–1
> - Groomsman won at 66–1
> - How's It Goin won at 7–1
>
> The accumulated winning odds of 3,072,887–1 were reported by Ladbrokes, who laid the bet, as a world record, and the punter's winnings came to £208,098.79 for an outlay of just over £5.
>
> Some mug!

Heinz

Combines six selections in fifty-seven bets:

- fifteen doubles
- twenty trebles
- fifteen four-horse accumulators

- six five-horse accumulators
- one six-horse accumulator.

Super Heinz

Combines seven selections in 120 bets:

- twenty-one doubles
- thirty-five trebles
- thirty-five four-horse accumulators
- twenty-one five-horse accumulators
- seven six-horse accumulators
- one seven-horse accumulator.

Goliath

Combines eight selections in 247 bets:

- twenty-eight doubles
- fifty-six trebles
- seventy four-horse accumulators
- fifty-six five-horse accumulators
- twenty-eight six-horse accumulators
- eight seven-horse accumulators
- one eight-horse accumulator.

Speciality bets

These apply to just one race and include:

Exacta

A Tote bet which involves giving the first and second horses in their correct finishing order. (The Tote Dual Forecast, which involved

Union Jack

As an example of the weird and wonderful contortions of betting in multiples, look no further than the Union Jack – the true nature of which can only be illustrated by reproducing the betting shop slip which accommodates this bet. You choose nine horses, combined in eight trebles:

selections 1,2,3
4,5,6
7,8,9
1,4,7
2,5,8
3,6,9
1,5,9
3,5,7

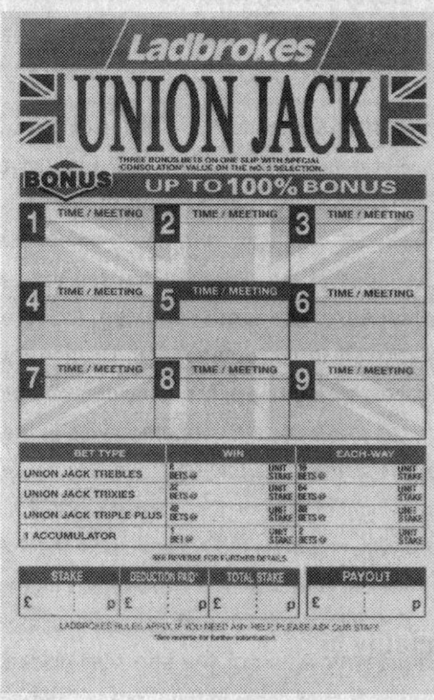

Ladbrokes

UNION JACK

BONUS UP TO 100% BONUS

1 TIME / MEETING	2 TIME / MEETING	3 TIME / MEETING
4 TIME / MEETING	5 TIME / MEETING	6 TIME / MEETING
7 TIME / MEETING	8 TIME / MEETING	9 TIME / MEETING

BET TYPE	WIN	EACH-WAY
UNION JACK TREBLES	BETS @ UNIT STAKE	BETS @ UNIT STAKE
UNION JACK TRIXIES	BETS @ UNIT STAKE	BETS @ UNIT STAKE
UNION JACK TRIPLE PLUS	BETS @ UNIT STAKE	BETS @ UNIT STAKE
1 ACCUMULATOR	1 BET @ UNIT STAKE	2 BETS @ UNIT STAKE

STAKE	DEDUCTION PAID	TOTAL STAKE	PAYOUT
£ p	£ p	£ p	£ p

Union Jack Trixies involve three doubles and one treble on each of the eight groups, making thirty-two bets, and a Union Jack Triple Plus combines your Union Jack Trebles with your Union Jack Trixies. Does all this make you yearn for a win single?

giving the first two horses in either order, has been discontinued. If you know which horses are going to finish first and second but don't know which will be first and which second, you need two Exacta bets – popularly known as a 'reverse forecast'.)

Computer Straight Forecast

A betting-shop wager (usually abbreviated to CSF) which involves predicting the first two in correct order. The bet is so

Heard that some horse is a racing certainty? Consider this . . .

At Chepstow on 28 June 1947 Glendower, ridden by Gordon Richards, started at 20–1 on to beat his solitary opponent, Markwell. This was in the days before starting stalls, and as the tapes of the old-style starting gate went up Glendower whipped round and unseated the great jockey, leaving Markwell to win unopposed. Gordon Richards related this embarrassing tale in his autobiography, adding: 'I heard afterwards that a certain gentleman was in the habit of picking out my best ride of the day, and then ringing up his bookmaker and backing it to win one thousand pounds. On that day he selected Glendower, but he did not anticipate that I would start at twenty to one on. That race cost him twenty thousand pounds.'

A salutary lesson for those ready to stake twenty grand. Yet Glendower was not the shortest-priced loser that Gordon Richards ever rode. In the Clarence House Stakes at Ascot on 23 September 1948 he partnered Royal Forest, who started at 25–1 on to beat three opponents (all 33–1 against) – one of whom, Burpham, beat the favourite half a length.

called because the dividend is calculated by computer, using a formula too complex for mortal man to comprehend.

Tricast

In handicaps of eight or more declared runners and no fewer than six actual runners, the punter must select the first three in correct order. Again, a computer calculates the dividend. (The Tote equivalent is the Trifecta – see page 94.)

The Tote

Betting with the Tote – the Horserace Totalisator Board – is based on a simple principle. All the money bet on all the horses in a race goes into a pot or 'pool'; following the race, this pool is shared out among all those who have placed winning bets.

The picture is complicated slightly by the deductions that are made from the pool before payout to cover running costs, including contributions to racecourses and to the Betting Levy.

There are separate pools for the different sorts of bet, and each pool is subjected to a different level of deduction. At the beginning of 2001 the deductions were:

- 16 per cent from the Win pool
- 24 per cent from the Place pool
- 29 per cent each from the Exacta, Jackpot and Trifecta
- 27 per cent from the Placepot
- 26 per cent from the Quadpot

A simple example will show how this works. Say the Win pool for a race consists of £10,000, of which one thousand £1 bets have been staked on the horse which wins:

pool	£10,000
deduction	£1,600
payout	£8,400
dividend	£8.40 per £1 ticket

The dividend (or 'Tote return') is declared to a £1 unit and includes the stake, so the actual winnings in the above example are £7.40. All the other pools operate in the same way as the Win pool.

The Tote screens at racecourses (and in those betting shops where you can have a direct Tote bet) will show you approximate Tote odds as the betting takes place before a race, but you cannot know exactly what the dividend will be until after the race, and this is the crucial difference between betting with the Tote and with a bookmaker: with a bookmaker you bet either at starting price or at the price which he quotes you or has displayed, and your bet remains at that price regardless of how many other people place bets after you, and at what odds; with the Tote you will not know when you make the bet precisely what the return will be, as it will be affected by all the people who place their bets after you. Off-course you have even less chance of seeing the likely return: it is not possible for the television viewer to know how the Tote odds are looking just before the race, and some off-course betting shops do not bet at Tote odds.

Because Tote and bookies operate on different principles, their odds usually differ; but neither side is consistently favoured by the discrepancy.

The Tote is a big player in British racing and a prominent presence as a race sponsor – notably of the Cheltenham Gold Cup, Chester Cup, Ebor Handicap, Cambridgeshire and Cesarewitch, Becher Chase, Tote Gold Trophy (formerly the Schweppes), Tote Northern National (formerly the Eider Chase) and – from 2001 – the Ayr Gold Cup. In all the Tote provides well over £2 million a year in race sponsorship.

The Tote's profits go back into racing.

Tote betting

Win

You bet on one horse to come first.

- The record win dividend was £341 2s 6d to a two-shilling stake on Coole at Haydock Park on 30 November 1929: the Tote odds of over 3,410–1 compared with a starting price of 100–8, or just over 12–1.

Place

You bet on a horse to be placed:

- first or second in races of five, six or seven runners;
- first, second or third in races of eight runners or more;
- first, second, third or fourth in handicaps of sixteen runners or more.

The record place dividend was £67.32 to 10p on Strip Fast (started 66–1), second in an apprentice race at Nottingham on 31 October 1978.

Exacta

In races of three or more runners, you pick two horses to finish first and second in the correct order.

Trifecta

You pick the first three home in the designated race in correct order – simplicity itself! Although a punter could make just one selection of three horses to finish 1, 2, 3, most prefer permutations: to perm the finishing orders of three horses requires six bets, four horses twenty-four bets, five horses sixty bets, and so on.

The first ever Trifecta, on the Vodafone Stewards' Cup at Goodwood on 1 August 1998, attracted a pool of £127,909, and the dividend for those gifted with second sight and nominating Superior Premium to beat Ansellman with Eastern Purple third was £6,311.00 to a £1 stake – compared with the bookmakers' Tricast on the same race paying £4,192.88.

Scoop6

The Scoop6 is a weekly Tote bet which every Saturday involves predicting the winners of six designated races, all of which are normally shown on Channel Four Racing. Money bet is pooled and distributed among the week's successful punters, who are then eligible to increase their winnings substantially by predicting the winner of the designated 'bonus race' the following Saturday. There is a consolation dividend for those who fail to come up with all six winners but manage to find six placed horses.

With a minimum bet of £2, the Scoop6 holds out the prospect of huge winnings from a very small outlay, and the excitement which builds up as punters go for the bonus can make for gripping television. Who could forget the scenes at Doncaster on St Leger day 2000 when Wayne Flanagan and his twenty-seven-strong stag party roared home Bound For Pleasure from an impossible position to a last-gasp triumph in that day's bonus race, the Ladbrokes.co.uk Handicap – landing the lads a cool £95,797 bonus to go with the £132,043 they had picked up by winning the Scoop6 the previous week? Or the joy of pensioner Jim Littlewood – once a stable lad with royal trainer Cecil Boyd-Rochfort – when The Extra Man landed the Tote Scoop6 Sandown Handicap Hurdle in February 2001 to net him a bonus of £76,103.20?

The post-race reaction of Wayne Flanagan's stag party at Doncaster summed up the appeal of the Scoop6. You have to be pretty overwhelmed to bear-hug Derek Thompson, even in the ecstasy of a victory like that and waiting through the stewards' enquiry, but when he had calmed down a little and disentangled himself from Tommo, Wayne observed: 'It's absolutely unreal. Twenty-seven lads came to a stag do [at Haydock Park the previous Saturday, when they won the Scoop6], and now they've got another stag do which has turned out even better than last week's.'

And another member of the stag party, Peter Callan, made an observation which could be the motto of Scoop6: 'Money talks. Normally it says goodbye to us, but today it's saying hello.'

Forecast / Exacta combinations

Bet to finish first and second in either order

selections	*number of bets*
3	6
4	12
5	20
6	30

Tote Trifecta

To finish first, second or third in any order

selections	*number of bets*
3	6
4	24
5	60
6	120
7	210
8	336

As with all pool betting, the key to the giant pay-out on the Scoop6 is that there should be as few winning tickets – and thus as few winning punters sharing the payout – as possible. If nobody wins, the money is carried over to the following week's pool.

Jackpot

All you have to do is pick the winners of the first six races at the designated Jackpot meeting. If there is no winner the pool is carried forward to the next Jackpot meeting.

- The record Jackpot dividend was £273,365.80 to £1 at Newmarket on 2 October 1993.

Placepot

You pick horses to be placed in the first six races (or, for any race with fewer than five runners, to win). The Placepot operates at all meetings.

- The record Placepot dividend was declared at Newmarket on 3 May 1998: £23,914.40 to a £1 stake.

Quadpot

You pick horses to be placed in the final four legs of the Placepot.

- The record Quadpot dividend was £2,119.30 to £1 at Ascot on 15 June 1994.

Tote Multibet

Double, treble, accumulator, Patent, Yankee, etc.

The year's big betting races

The major bookmaking firms publish lists of the races which provide the greatest amount of betting turnover. For Ladbrokes, largest bookmaker in Britain, the top twenty races in 2000, by turnover, were:

1 Martell Grand National (Aintree) *BBC*
2 Vodafone Derby (Epsom Downs) *Channel Four*
3 Tote Cheltenham Gold Cup (Cheltenham) *Channel Four*
4 Ladbroke Scottish National (Ayr) *Channel Four*
5 Sagitta Two Thousand Guineas (Newmarket) *Channel Four*
6 Pertemps King George VI Chase (Kempton Park) *Channel Four*
7 Whitbread Gold Cup (Sandown Park) *Channel Four*
8 Worthington Lincoln Handicap (Doncaster) *Channel Four*
9 Tote Cambridgeshire (Newmarket) *Channel Four*
10 Racing Post Chase (Kempton Park) *Channel Four*
11 Vodafone Stewards' Cup (Goodwood) *BBC*
12 Hennessy Cognac Gold Cup (Newbury) *BBC*
13 Vodafone Oaks (Epsom Downs) *Channel Four*
14 Irish Independent Arkle Trophy (Cheltenham) *Channel Four*
15 Tote International Handicap (Ascot) *BBC*
16 Tote Gold Trophy (Newbury) *BBC*
17 Wokingham Handicap (Ascot) *BBC*
18 Dubai Champion Stakes (Newmarket) *Channel Four*
19 William Hill Handicap Chase (Cheltenham) *Channel Four*
20 Coral-Eclipse Stakes (Sandown Park) *Channel Four*

Of these twenty, fourteen were shown live on Channel Four Racing.

VARIATIONS AND COMPLICATIONS

Ante-post betting

Ante-post betting – wagering on an event well in advance of its taking place – provides the potential for lashings of value: provided, that is, that your selection actually gets to the start of the race.

Bets on the very big races – the Grand National, the first four Classics, the Cheltenham Gold Cup, Champion Hurdle and Triumph Hurdle – are being struck months before, while most of the big handicaps on the Flat (notably the Lincoln, Stewards' Cup, Cambridgeshire and Cesarewitch) attract lively markets for several weeks before they are actually run.

If you are exceptionally clairvoyant, you can even bet years in advance, provided you can get someone to take the bet. In 1967 the famous bookmaker William Hill laid owner Raymond Guest £50,000 to £500 (100–1) against an as yet unraced two-year-old winning the Derby the following year (and, for good measure, £12,500 to £500 the place): the horse was Sir Ivor, who won the Derby easily under Lester Piggott in 1968. The starting price was 5–4 on.

Another unraced two-year-old was the subject of a wondrous ante-post bet in 1986. Derek Powley, manager of the Cliveden Stud, got odds of 500–1 that a colt who had been foaled at the stud the previous year would win the

John McCririck's top tips on ante-post betting

Bookmakers claim that they lose on ante-post betting, and that it's principally window-dressing, but from the punter's point of view it can provide a great deal of fun. Even a poor man like me can have his moments, and the memory is still strong of how an ante-post voucher on Zafonic for the 1993 Two Thousand Guineas, acquired at Longchamp the day Khalid Abdullah's great colt romped away with the Prix de la Salamandre, gave me a rosy glow all that winter – and Zafonic did not let me down at Newmarket, charging home at 6–5 on, a good deal skinnier price than I had on my ante-post voucher. If only ante-post were always that straightforward!

But a few words of ante-post advice:

- Be wary of a long-distance ante-post punt on a horse whose chances might be diminished by extremes of going: you cannot tell far in advance that he'll have conditions in his favour on the day.
- Be careful about serious ante-post betting in a race where the draw is known to be a significant factor, such as the Lincoln Handicap or the Ayr Gold Cup.
- The more inside knowledge you have about running plans the better. Be as sure as you can be that the horse is actually being aimed at the race in question.
- Remember that wisest of old betting sayings: 'You can't go skint taking a profit.' If the horse you've backed ante-post at

continued opposite

1987 Derby, and the horse did just that: Reference Point, starting price 6–4.

A more recent example of exceptionally far-sighted backing revolves around 1997 One Thousand Guineas winner Sleepytime, who when an unnamed yearling two years earlier had been backed by those in the know to win that Classic.

It can work the other way. In May 1986 a man walked into a West Country betting shop and asked for a price about an as yet unnamed four-month-old foal by Mill Reef out of 1983 Arc winner All Along winning the 1989 Derby. Quoted 500–1, he forked out £300 on the nose. Along All (as the foal was named) kept the punter's hope alive through an encouraging juvenile career in France, but never got to run in the 1989 Derby.

The great advantage of ante-post betting is of course that you can get very much better odds than the horse will start at – though this is not guaranteed: the horse's price may lengthen. The great disadvantage is that you lose your money

50–1 shortens to 6–4 favourite, you could theoretically lay that horse at 2–1 yourself and be guaranteed a profit. Theoretically – but not legally, unless you have a bookmaker's licence. When you find yourself the happy possessor of a 50–1 voucher about a 6–4 chance, make the most of it by backing other horses in the race.

- Don't throw away your voucher as soon as the horse is withdrawn. If the race is abandoned (and even the Derby was threatened in 1983), all ante-post bets are refunded.

if the horse is withdrawn before the race. (But note this: if your horse is withdrawn but the race is abandoned you get your money back, for you cannot lose on an event which does not happen.)

Sometimes bookmakers will offer ante-post odds 'with a run' – that is, if the horse does not take part your money is returned. All the 'Will she? Won't she?' speculation buzzing around Cape Verdi before her connections decided whether she would take on the colts in the 1998 Vodafone Derby meant that in the weeks between her One Thousand Guineas victory and the announcement that she would run she made an extremely dubious ante-post proposition, as the likelihood that she would miss the Derby and go instead for the more natural target the Vodafone Oaks remained live. Once it was decided that she would take on the colts, order was restored to the Derby ante-post market – but punters who had backed her for the Oaks before her mightily impressive win at Newmarket, many when she was a two-year-old, took great umbrage that she missed that race and thus denied them of the opportunity of a nice touch.

Betting tax

If you make a bet off-course – say in a betting shop – you will be liable to a tax (usually 9 per cent) on the transaction. Tax can be

- added to your stake – so that a £5 bet 'tax paid' would actually cost you £5.45 but you would have no deduction from your returns in the event of winning; or
- deducted from your return (that is, winnings plus returned stake): so if you had a £5 winning bet at

> 10–1 and did not bet 'tax paid', handing over just the fiver, your actual return – the amount you would collect – would be £50.95 (£50 winnings plus £5 stake less £4.95, 9 per cent of the total).

You pays your money and you takes your choice, but it is worth being aware of the effect of tax on very short-priced winners. A £10 winning bet at evens, without tax paid at the time of making the bet, returns £18.20, a profit on the transaction of just £8.20. The same bet tax paid on would return a profit of £9.10 – work it out! A bet of £10 to win, tax not paid on, which comes in at 2–1 on brings a return of just £13.65. The same bet on-course, where there is no betting tax, would give you a return of £15. But remember! Betting duty is to be abolished from the beginning of 2002.

Rule 4

Betting is regulated by rules laid down by the Tattersalls Committee. Rule 4 addresses the problem of the distortions in the betting market which occur if one (or more) of the runners is withdrawn shortly before the race – for example, when a horse refuses to enter the starting stalls: betting will have started in earnest on that race and there may be no time to make a new book. In such instances, money staked on the horse withdrawn is returnable to the punters. The shorter the price of that horse at the time of withdrawal, the greater the distortion of the market, so Rule 4 sets out a scale whereby a deduction is made from all winning bets in that race, the size of the deduction depending on the price of the withdrawn horse at the time of withdrawal.

Rule 4 also applies when a horse is deemed by the starter not to have taken part in the race – for instance, if a horse whips round at a tape start and refuses to race.

The scale of deductions is as follows:

price	*deduction (p in the £)*
30–100 (or shorter)	75
2–5 to 1–3	70
8–15 to 4–9	65
8–13 to 4–7	60
4–5 to 4–6	55
20–21 to 5–6	50
evens to 6–5	45
5–4 to 6–4	40
13–8 to 7–4	35
15–8 to 9–4	30
5–2 to 3–1	25
100–30 to 4–1	20
9–2 to 11–2	15
6–1 to 9–1	10
10–1 to 14–1	5
15–1 and over	no deduction

Note: Rule 4 also applies with spread betting (see pages 110–14).

Dead heat

In the case of a dead heat the punter receives the full odds to half the stake. So £5 to win on a horse which started at 10–1 and dead-heated for first place would return £27.50 – winnings of £25 plus the return of half the stake (£2.50).

No starting price

When Dancing Brave turned out for his Arc prep race at Goodwood in September 1986 he was such a total, stone-bonking certainty to beat his five opponents that course bookmakers could muster no interest in betting on the result of the race. When such races happen (they occasionally do) no starting prices are returned. All bets struck are void.

Betting on overseas races

Time was when the only occasion a British punter might think about having a bet on an overseas race was on the first Sunday in October, and the perennial question would come up: is it better to back your fancy for the Prix de l'Arc de Triomphe at odds advertised by the bookies at home, or go for the on-track price offered by the Pari-Mutuel – the French tote monopoly?

Nowadays racing is increasingly international, with British horses regularly making forays to the top races abroad – not only in France and Ireland, but further afield in North America (where the Breeders' Cup has transformed the shape of the racing year), Dubai, Japan and even Australia (whose Melbourne Cup is now frequently a target for adventurous British and Irish trainers).

Bookmakers will usually advertise prices about the major overseas races – in some cases, such as the Arc, there will be a lively ante-post market – so the punter has a choice between taking those prices or betting at the locally returned prices, which are usually (as in France or the United States) Pari-Mutuel or tote prices.

The difference between bookmakers' and Pari-Mutuel prices can be spectacular. When Tolomeo – trained at Newmarket by Luca Cumani and ridden by Pat Eddery – won the Arlington Million in Chicago in 1983 he was priced as low as 6–1 by British layers, but the horse was little known in America and paid 38.2–1 on the track.

Betting terms in the USA

With racing from the USA becoming increasingly familiar to punters in the UK, not only on account of regular broadcasts of the Breeders' Cup but with a generally higher level of television coverage of American racing, it may be useful to have a brief explanation of the main betting terms in that country. Remember that all American on-course betting is carried out on a pari-mutuel – pool – basis.

Win Back the horse to win.
Place Back the horse to come first or second.
Show Back the horse to come first, second or third (assuming the number of runners allows for a payout on the third horse).
Exacta Pick the first two finishers in correct order. (Also called a perfecta.)
Trifecta Pick the first three in correct order.
Quinella Pick the first two finishers in either order.
Pick Three, Pick Six, Pick Nine Bets in which the winners of all the included races must be selected.

Such bonanza payouts are becoming rarer as overseas punters get more used to seeing British raiders in their races, and today there is less likelihood of a horse with a real chance being ignored in the local betting: when Dancing Brave ran in the Breeders' Cup Turf at Santa Anita in 1986, he went off the 2–1 on favourite – but still lost.

Lays and Bismarcks

Since betting on horses is essentially a matter of pitching the punter's opinion against the bookmaker's, it is an invaluable part of the punting armoury to be able to second-guess the bookie. If you know that he is willing to 'lay' a horse, to take money for that runner in the expectation that it will not win, you will want to know why – and take his opposition either as a warning signal or as an opportunity for some decent value.

John McCririck's 'Lay of the Day', which began in early 1998 and was intended to highlight fancied horses who should be opposed, merely turned up an embarrassing succession of winners, culminating in Martin Pipe's Blowing Wind, 5–1 favourite when landing the Sunderlands Imperial Cup at Sandown Park in March. Having kissed the feet of trainer Martin Pipe in the Sandown winner's enclosure, Big Mac announced the early demise of Lay of the Day: 'I keep on saying I'm a man who can hardly tip a loser, so I'm out of it now. It just shows why I'm a failed bookmaker.'

Cue a real professional in the shape of bookmaker Barry Dennis. Barry's weekly telephonic presence on *The Morning Line* (occasionally dripping straight from the shower or, in February 2001, calling from the cricket ground in Sri Lanka where he was watching England lose the test match) became a feature of the Saturday morning show, and an invaluable insight into how a top bookmaker assesses a race. For example, that day Barry called from Sri Lanka, his Bismarck (*Sink the Bismarck* – geddit?) was Hail The Chief, predicted odds-on favourite in the morning papers for his race at Lingfield but a horse whose real chance, in the opinion of Barry Dennis, was far shakier than those odds suggested. Sure enough, Hail The Chief was an uneasy favourite in the Lingfield ring when on-course betting on the race opened, and could finish only second. Another successful failure chalked up to Barry's Bismarcks.

In weighing up a race, it's as vital to know why individual horses might not win as why they might.

Betting on sport – and beyond

Few punters confine themselves purely to horse racing (or horses and greyhounds), and the last few years have seen a huge increase in the level of sports betting: the 1998 World Cup in France was described as 'the planet's biggest betting event' by Graham Sharpe of William Hill; industry-wide, the competition reportedly produced a betting turnover of £120 million. It also, again according to William Hill, twice broke the record for the biggest bet ever placed: one punter had £200,000 on England to beat Colombia at 5–4 on (thereby winning £160,000), and the same high-roller had £240,000 on Brazil to beat France in the final (thereby returning his earlier winnings – and more).

As evidence of the growth of sports betting, a random glance at the back pages of a Saturday edition of the *Racing*

Post early in 2001 revealed betting on tennis, Rugby Union, football, American football, cricket, bowls, boxing, snooker, golf and Rugby League – in all sorts of competitions in all sorts of countries.

There has also been a surge in betting on non-sporting outcomes, such as political events – and other less orthodox contests. When in 1990 senior clerics entered the stalls – choir rather than starting – for the race to be next Archbishop of Canterbury, George Carey started out the 20–1 'rag', then attracted suspiciously heavy betting just before the off: Ladbrokes took £2,000 for him on the very morning of the announcement. Carey duly came in, whereupon dark rumours started circulating that the bookmakers had been stitched up by ecclesiastical insiders in the know . . .

Then there is a wholly daft vein of betting which attracts huge media attention on account of its sheer zaniness. In recent years William Hill have quoted such mouth-watering odds as

- 10,000–1 that a UFO would land on top of the Millennium Dome at Greenwich some time during the year 2000;
- 2,000–1 that Elvis Presley will be proved to be still alive;
- 500–1 a positive sighting of the Loch Ness Monster.

But even these bets are not as bizarre as that sought by the punter who some years ago contacted Ron Pollard, Ladbrokes' renowned odds guru, and asked for a price about the actress Mae West being shown on her death to have been a man all along.

SPREAD BETTING

Fixed-odds betting, however baffling it may appear at first sight to the uninitiated, is simplicity itself compared with spread betting. This novel form of punting, pioneered by companies such as Sporting Index and City Index, grew rapidly throughout the 1990s and is now an integral part of the betting scene.

The essence of spread betting is wagering on a range – a 'spread' – of possibilities. Most sporting events are decided by numbers – runs in cricket, goals in soccer, points in rugby – and the spread better backs his or her view on what those numbers will be. So if the spread-betting firm is of the opinion that the total number of points scored in a rugby international will be 29, it may quote '28–30'. If you think the match will produce more points than 29, you 'buy' at 30; if fewer than 29, you 'sell' at 28. The punter makes the decision to buy (the higher figure) or sell (the lower) and stipulates the stake, but here's the rub: your profit or loss on the bet is calculated by measuring the difference between the price at which you bought or sold and the actual result, and multiplying your stake by that figure. So, unlike in fixed-odds betting, your losses are not confined to the amount you have staked. If you buy the spread at £10 a point and the total number of points is 25, you lose £50: 30 minus 25 equals 5. But if you sell the spread at £10 a point and the total number of points is 25, you win £30 (28 minus 25).

All very interesting, but what has this to do with horse racing? Applications of spread betting in racing have included such matters as

- how many runners will complete the course in the Grand National;
- the total winning distances at an individual race meeting;
- performances of favourites at a meeting, with market leaders scoring points on an advertised scale;
- the distance by which one named horse will beat another, wherever they actually finish in the race;
- betting on the jockeys' index: back or oppose your selected jockey, so that every ride he has on the card is running for you;
- favourites: back or oppose the favourites for a whole programme without having to pick which horse will actually win.

As with fixed-odds betting, the spread changes with circumstances – and, in the case of most sports, during the event itself.

One of the attractions of spread betting is that you can back your opinion if you think the horse in question will lose, as well as if you think he will win. Another is that the more right you are, the more money you will win. The danger, of course, is that the more wrong you are, the more you will lose (though in bets such as those relating to distance a ceiling is usually imposed).

Two other points to remember. You cannot have a spread bet in a betting shop or on the racecourse – only through an

continued on page 114

Spread betting on the 2000 King George VI Chase

As an example of how spread betting applies to horse racing, this is the spread advertised by Sporting Index (one of the longest-established spread betting companies) for the Pertemps King George VI Chase at Kempton Park on Boxing Day 2000:

See More Business	26–29
First Gold	18–21
Florida Pearl	10–13
Beau	6–8
Edredon Bleu	5–7
Lady Cricket	4–6
Go Ballistic	3–5
Bellator	1–3
Double Thriller	1–3

winner 50 points
second 25 points
third 10 points

Say you 'bought' See More Business for £10. The gelding finished only fifth, thereby scoring no points on the advertised scale, so you lose 29 times your stake: £290. Had he won, you would have netted 21 (50 points for winning, less the 29 of the spread) times your stake: £210. Had he come second, you would have lost £40 (29 minus 25 equals 4). On the other hand, had you taken a dim view of See More Business's chance, figuring that he would finish unplaced, you could have 'sold' him, in which case a £10 unit would have won you £260 – 26 times your stake.

To illustrate the perils and possibilities of spread betting, compare the See More Business spread bet with what would have happened had you had a tenner on the horse at his starting price of 6–4: maximum loss £10, possible winnings £15.

Sporting Index also advertised match bets. A match expressed as

See More Business / First Gold
2.5 – 4.0
Max M/u 15 lengths

concerns the number of lengths by which See More Business will beat First Gold, or vice versa. If you think See More Business will beat First Gold you buy at 4. When in the King George itself First Gold beats See More Business by 31 lengths the maximum make-up ('Max M/u') applies, restricting your loss to 19 times your stake – the 15 of the maximum make-up plus the 4 of the spread at which you bought. If you think First Gold will beat See More Business, you sell at 2.5, and when First Gold comes home 31 lengths ahead of the other horse you win 17.5 times your stake – the maximum make-up of 15 lengths plus the 2.5 at which you sold.

Simple, huh?

account with one of the spread bookmakers. And if you get it so comprehensively wrong that you cannot afford to pay up, beware: unlike with orthodox betting, you can be sued for the debt by your bookmaker. (And he, should it come to it, can be sued by you.)

A simple way of remembering the key difference in spread betting between buying and selling is that you *buy* to go *big*, and *sell* to go *small* – or remember that *buy* is *high*.

GETTING ON

There are four ways to place a bet on a horse race:

- on the racecourse
- in a betting shop
- through a telephone account with a bookmaker
- over the internet.

On the racecourse

'Five to four the field ... I'll lay six to four ... sixes bar one ...'

Bookmakers shouting the odds provide a British racecourse with its unique sound, a babble of noise which at first may sound like gibberish but on closer attention reveals business being transacted swiftly between layers and punters.

When a bookmaker shouts 'five to four the field' (which usually sounds like 'fidah vaudeville') he – occasionally she – is indicating that 5–4 is the shortest price he has on offer; 'I'll take six to four' means he is offering 6–4 on, while 'I'll lay six to four' means 6–4 against; 'sixes bar one' means that he is offering all the runners in the race except one at 6–1 or longer.

The principal betting ring at most racecourses is in 'Tatts' – the Tattersalls enclosure, named after the company which in 1866 drew up the first rules on betting transactions. (The Tattersalls Committee is still recognized as the body with authority to settle all disputes relating to bets, and has the power to 'warn off' – that is, ban from racecourses – an individual for non-payment.)

Betting with bookmakers is not usually allowed in the Members' enclosure, so the larger companies have representatives who maintain a position by the rail dividing Members from Tatts, and take bets – some in cash, many in credit – from the members on the other side of it. Much of the serious punting is done here with these 'rails bookmakers', though it is only very recently that rails bookies have been allowed to display their prices on boards like Tatts bookmakers: hitherto they were confined to shouting the odds.

In the main betting ring bookmakers are allotted pitches according to seniority. Smart new pitch equipment which became mandatory a couple of years ago means that the days of a bookmaker's business being characterised by a wizened old satchel, a scarcely less wizened old clerk making entries in a huge ledger and the layer himself dispensing brightly coloured betting tickets are now behind us. Instead the modern racecourse bookmaker is equipped with up-to-date technology. Laptop computers have replaced the old ledgers to give an up-to-the-second account of the bookies' liabilities, while those familiar and much-loved brightly coloured tickets have been replaced by a computer-generated receipt which names the horse and the bet, and states the return you will receive if the bet is a winning one.

Having begun betting from the 'tissue', the course bookmaker adjusts the odds according to the flow of money until the race is started, at which point a team of official starting price reporters agree on what is to be the officially returned starting price (SP) for each horse. To arrive at these, they note the prices available in the ring, and if there are significant discrepancies will often split the difference. So if approximately a quarter of the principal layers have the favourite at 5–4 at the off, half are offering 6–5 and others go 11–10 or evens the same horse, the officially returned starting price is likely to be 6–5. The same process explains weird SPs like 85–40 (halfway between 2–1 and 9–4).

Some people are put off betting in the ring by the sheer level of activity – all that hustle and bustle as punters search around for the best price, then panic as they see it start to go before they've got on, and push and shove to get to the last bookie showing those odds – only to see him wipe it off the board just as they reach his pitch. ('It's on my finger' has sometimes been the snide retort, while wiping the chalk away on his trousers.) But the brave are rewarded with the fun of being part of that seething mass of activity, and the actual transaction is perfectly straightforward.

The bookmaker displays his odds on a board, constantly revising them as the market shifts by wiping them off and writing up fresh ones. When you see a bookmaker showing against the name of your fancy the price at which you want to bet, go up, offer the money and state the bet you want – giving the racecard number of the horse, not the name (though it would be a pretty slow-witted bookmaker who could not quickly identify that horse on his board if you did not know the number).

Say you're at Newcastle for the Tote Northern National in February 2001 and you want to back Seven Towers in the big race. A bookmaker is showing the horse at 7–1, which you consider a reasonable price. You note Seven Towers's number from the racecard – 4 – approach the bookmaker's joint and

*FUTUREBET 2000*BOOKMAKER'S TICKET 416 250

PAUL GALE
Northern BPA Leeds LS15 8AJ

* R 5 new 17-02-01
10.00 WIN
4 SEVEN TOWE 7/1

W: 80.00

say simply '£10 to win number 4', or '£70 to £10 number 4'. You give him a tenner, he calls the bet to his clerk as 'seventy pounds to ten number 4' and gives you the computerised receipt (above) which records details of that bet. Check those details before leaving the joint.

Seven Towers could manage no better than a fast-finishing third in the Tote Northern National, but had he won you would have returned to that bookmaker, presented your ticket and been given the £80 recorded on your receipt – your £10 stake returned and £70 winnings.

The main on-course alternative to betting with a bookmaker is to bet with the Tote.

This is an altogether more orderly experience. You go to any Tote window, state the racecard number of the horse, the type of bet you want (see pages 93–4 above) and the amount to be staked, and hand over your money. You will be given a receipt for your bet (check it before leaving the window, as

tote RACECOURSE DIVISION tote

NCSTLE 17\02\2001
RACE 5 15:39:33
Stake: 5.00

WIN

Selections
8. Royal Tommy

TOTAL: 5.00

W\N 2010 D\C 3876
8450-3A04-1A96-A001

PLEASE CHECK YOUR TICKETS!

Tote receipt for a £5 win bet on Royal Tommy in the Tote Northern National, 17 February 2001.

even the Tote's famous Ladies in Red are only human). If you win, return to any Tote window – it doesn't have to be the one where you placed the bet – present your ticket, and you'll be paid. Simple!

Betting shops

Today there are about 8,000 betting shops in Britain, responsible for a large proportion of the £5,000 million bet off-course every year. Forty years ago there weren't any at all. Until 1 May 1961, when the first betting shops in Great Britain were opened, betting on horses could legally be done only on a racecourse or through a credit account. Illegally, it was done all over the place, with 'bookies' runners' operating in pubs and clubs and on street corners; and it was in an attempt to stamp out this illicit activity that Home Secretary R. A. 'Rab' Butler introduced the Betting and Gaming Act that made betting shops possible.

Legal was one thing; attractive was another entirely. Butler noted in his memoirs that 'the House of Commons was so intent on making betting shops as sad as possible, in order not to deprave the young, that they ended up more like undertakers' premises'. Indeed, for decades betting shops laboured under a reputation as seedy and uninviting places fostered by the regulations on their operation – they were not allowed to show races live on television or offer light refreshments to their patrons; but after a couple of decades of stumbling on in the gloom, a less censorious approach won through.

New legislation passed in 1986 allowed a general brightening up of betting shops and, most significantly, the transmission of races live on television from Satellite Information Services. Even coffee machines appeared. At last, the notion of a betting shop as an establishment into which no respectable person should ever stray unless under extreme duress, in which case the experience should be as shaming and uncomfortable as possible to discourage its repetition, had at last disappeared. Now, with evening opening and Sunday opening, betting shops have become respectable outposts of the leisure industry, a move accelerated early in 1995 when they were at last allowed to show their interiors to high-street passers-by, rather than skulking guiltily behind solid display boards in the shop windows.

Nevertheless, despite their more inviting demeanour these days, to some folk betting shops still have the magnetic but intimidating aura of the brothel; so, for would-be clients still shy about entering such a place, it may be helpful to explain how you have a bet.

Around the walls are displayed a large array of newspapers and television screens giving all sorts of information on the day's sport. When you've decided what you want to back, take a carbon-backed slip from one of the dispensers on the counters all round the shop – different sorts of bet require different slips – and write on it the details of your bet. (Ballpoint pens are thoughtfully provided for the purpose.) It is essential that you fill in this slip accurately: if you had got confused and had a fiver on Florida Gold for the 2000 Pertemps King George VI Chase at Kempton Park, you would have had no right to feel aggrieved if the bookmaker called the bet void and declined to pay out on First Gold (how was he to know you did not really mean runner-up Florida Pearl?), and all sorts of disputes arise from wrongly or ambiguously filled-in slips, or slips placing some highly elaborate combination wager when the amount staked does not cover the bets involved.

The slip itself (see page 122) is not very difficult. For a win bet you would just need to enter the name of the horse, the time of the race and the course where it is to be run, and the amount you wish to stake. (You also have the option to have the bet 'tax paid', which means that you pay the betting tax on the stake: see page 102.) You give the slip and your money to the assistant behind the counter, who will time-stamp the slip in a machine and return the bottom copy to you. You then, according to your constitution, either hang around nonchalantly as your horse sweeps to victory on the screen or scurry off to shout and perspire in the privacy of your own home, and when the 'weighed-in' signal is given saunter to the payout end of the counter to collect your winnings.

Remember that if you have not bet 'tax paid' 9 per cent will be taken off your returns.

The unquenchable optimism of the punter: a betting shop slip for a fiver (tax paid) on eternal loser Quixall Crossett for his ninety-ninth race – and ninety-ninth defeat – at Kelso, 1 February 2001.

Accounts

If you're going to bet off-course, you can give yourself a much more leisurely time of it by opening an account with a bookmaker. No more scuttling down to the betting shop during the adverts or placing all your bets in advance of the afternoon's transmission; you can bet by telephone at the very last minute, enabling you to make full use of the wisdom of the Channel Four Racing team as they discuss the runners in each race and to form your own judgements of how the horses behave in the preliminaries and go down to the start before you commit yourself.

It is easy to open an account: all the major credit firms advertise in the racing press. You'll need to decide what sort of account you want – whether a deposit account, whereby you deposit a sum of money with the bookmaker (probably not less than £100 with the big firms) and can bet until that amount is used up, or a credit account, where you are allowed credit up to an agreed limit. The introduction of accounts using Switch cards makes the debit of money from your bank account – when you lose – immediate, so you won't be building up huge debts.

You will be sent a statement regularly – very occasionally this will be accompanied by a cheque – and you can use your credit account with these firms' representatives at race meetings: Tote Credit, with 50,000 clients, has a special office on all courses.

Betting on the internet

Once the bookmaking fraternity appreciated the potential of the internet for growing its business by providing another means of placing a bet – and, through basing operations outside the UK, making internet betting tax-free – the profusion of betting opportunities over the web grew rapidly. The Big Three bookmakers – Ladbrokes, William Hill and Coral – have all established internet betting sites, and these have been joined not only by other sites on which you can place what might be called an 'orthodox' bet in the customary way, but by sites which offer additional ways of betting.

Once you are familiar with the means of accessing the web, getting into the swing of placing a bet is fairly straightforward – or should be.

First you need to enrol yourself as a member of a site and to establish a way of paying for losing bets and receiving the money from winning ones. The registration process can be maddening: the site will decline your patronage without making any suggestion of how you should register properly, or wait until you've told it all sorts of personal details and your mother's maiden name, before it remembers to tell you that it only accepts Switch cards that you do not have. Sites require details of a credit card or debit card to and from which they can transfer money, and once yours has been accepted (and assuming they don't take exception to your mother's maiden name) you can bet.

You click on to the event in which you're interested, consider the odds on offer, and click to bet. Having done so, you're given ample opportunity to change your mind as confirmation of the bet comes up on the screen, and often when you confirm the wager your electronic friend somewhere out in the ether will send you a cheery 'Good luck!'

If you are betting regularly you will need to monitor your account balance, though you will be reminded soon enough if you try to place a bet without having sufficient cover in your means of paying.

The great boon of internet betting from the point of view of television viewers is that you can wait until the very last minute – indeed, until the Channel Four Racing team have unburdened themselves of the Eyecatchers – before placing your bet, a facility previously available only to the small proportion of viewers who have a telephone betting account (or the even smaller proportion who live above a betting shop).

A disadvantage is that if you're mistrustful of electronic technology you don't have the reassurance of a paper receipt for your bet, nor the comforting voice of the telephone operator at the other end of the phone.

Alongside betting on horse racing, most sites offer a huge range of prices on other sports.

Addresses of some of the major on-line betting sites include

Ladbrokes: www.ladbrokes.co.uk
Bluesquare: www.bluesq.com
Coral Eurobet: www.eurobet.co.uk
Tote: www.totalbet.com
William Hill: www.williamhill.co.uk
Victor Chandler: www.victorchandler.co.uk
BetDirect: www.betdirect.net
Stanley Racing: www.stanleybet.co.uk

Other intriguing betting developments have been made possible by internet betting. For example, there are sites which match an individual punter against an individual layer. Say that in March 2001 you want to back Nayef for the

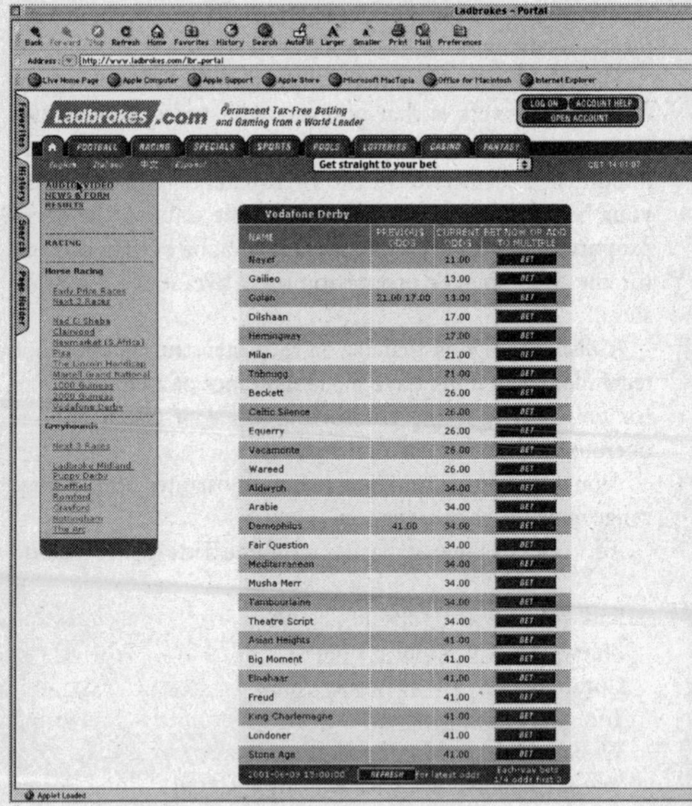

Ante-post betting for the 2001 Vodafone Derby on the Ladbrokes internet site. Note that the 'Current Odds' column displays potential returns to a £1 stake, rather than giving the odds in the traditional way: thus Nayef's ante-post price is 10–1, Galileo 12–1, Golan is in to 12–1 from 20–1 and 16–1, and so on. To strike your bet you click on the appropriate 'BET' box on the right, and away you go!

Vodafone Derby in June, but think that the prevailing odds of around 10–1 or 12–1 are a little skinny. Is there anyone out there who will lay you 16–1? On some sites you can pose that very question and wait to be accommodated – and you can do the same for much humbler races on a day-to-day basis. Sites who provide this sort of service include

Betfair: www.betfair.com
Flutter: www.flutter.com
Betswap: www.betswap.com
Betexchange: www.betexchange.co.uk

Such sites do not offer identical services: visit each before deciding whether it suits your requirements.

One very useful port of call for anyone about to place an internet bet is Oddschecker (www.oddschecker.co.uk), a mine of useful information comparing odds from different layers on a wide array of sports and events, highlighting horses going in and out in the betting, comparing the ease of use and conditions of various on-line betting sites, and a wealth of other material.

The *Racing Post* publishes an excellent weekly column called 'Net Prophet' which describes new sites, evaluates existing ones, and generally keeps you abreast of developments in this rapidly changing area of the betting world.

SYSTEMS

Betting systems provide a sort of template for your punting, a framework that dictates how and when you put your money on. Not many people bet only according to a system, but most regular punters have a few schemes they like to bear in mind, from supposedly logical notions such as backing the top weight in a nursery (a handicap for two-year-olds), on the basis that it is demonstrably the best horse in the race, to wholly illogical ones such as betting on greys or on a horse whose racecard number coincides with the date of Granny's birthday.

Among the most regularly followed systems are:

- backing favourites (around a third of all races are won by the market leader, but you won't make a profit out of backing them blindly);
- blindly backing horses ridden by a particular jockey (sometimes it works, sometimes it doesn't; had you staked £1 on every one of champion jockey Kevin Darley's 997 rides during the 2000 Flat season you would have backed 155 winners, but ended the year £209.83 down);
- backing particular trainers at particular courses – e.g. Martin Pipe at any of the West Country tracks.

John McCririck's top twelve betting systems

If there were a system that worked, everyone would have twigged by now. But it does no harm to have a few which might throw up the odd winner, and these are the ones I would recommend:

- Back the horse that won the same race last year. Many of the relevant factors – type of race, course, distance, time of year – are in its favour.
- Back horses blinkered or visored for the first time.
- Back the outsider of three. There's more logic to this than might be apparent at first, as races with very small fields are often run at a false pace, making a less predictable result more likely, and when punters concentrate on the first two in the betting there may be value to be had from the outsider.
- If a top jockey is riding at his absolute minimum weight, back his horse. He wouldn't have given up even his meagre breakfast if the creature had no chance!
- In handicaps, restrict yourself to horses running off their old mark when their new rating will be higher. (See pages 51–4.) They are clearly improving, and should be caught before their official reassessment is dictating the weight they carry.

continued overleaf

- In amateur and apprentice races, go for the most experienced and best jockey, whatever he or she is riding.
- Consider the effect of the draw sensibly. If a race is run on extremes of going and the draw has a marked effect, concentrate on the favoured side for all bets, including forecasts.
- When studying a maiden race, find out whether any of the runners are engaged in big races later in the season: those that are must be highly rated by connections.
- Back the animal whose stable has sent it the longest distance for the race.
- If a stable has more than one runner in a race, go for the outsider. They won't come in too often, but when they do rewards can be great.
- Totally illogically, support horses with the same initials in forecasts.
- And, just as bad, go for any horse whose racecard number is the same as its starting stall position.

But never get hooked on a system. It removes the flexibility – and a lot of the fun – from your punting. And whatever you do, don't forget that telegram wired home by the roulette player: 'System working well – send more money!'

WINNERS AND LOSERS

While it is impossible to be precise about exactly how much is wagered on a particular horse, some bets have become fabled.

Catching them early

Here's a handful of cases to inspire Channel Four Racing viewers thinking of having a cool twenty thou on their fancy:

Nashwan in the 1989 Two Thousand Guineas

Available at 33–1 only a few weeks before the race after an encouraging but not earth-shattering two-year-old career, Nashwan was backed steadily as reports came out of trainer Dick Hern's yard that the imposing chestnut had turned in a phenomenal gallop. In the words of Brough Scott in the *Racing Post*, 'all sorts of quite sane and sensible people around the Hern camp began to mutter behind their hands and shake at the knees.' They managed to control those knees enough to wobble down to the betting shop, and by the day of the race Nashwan's price had tumbled: Ladbrokes alone laid the colt to lose £250,000. Starting 3–1 favourite, Nashwan devoured the Rowley Mile to win from Exbourne and then go on to land the Derby at 5–4.

Noel Furlong at the 1991 Cheltenham Festival

You win some, you lose some, and on the opening day of the Cheltenham National Hunt Festival in March 1991 Irish owner, carpet magnate and fearless punter Noel Furlong did both. In September 1985 Furlong had fallen foul of Customs and Excise over supposedly unpaid VAT in the UK, and jumping bail and slipping over to Dublin made a visit to Cheltenham a trifle inadvisable until the matter was settled. Eventually Furlong came to an accommodation with Customs and Excise and was free to go to Cheltenham for his famous two-pronged tilt at the ring.

The first prong was Destriero, who had won a maiden hurdle at Leopardstown the previous December but was not seen out between then and the Supreme Novices' Hurdle, opening race of the Festival. 'We didn't want to run him because we didn't want to end up getting 2–1 instead of 6–1' was Furlong's explanation for Destriero's absence from the track, and on the day that 6–1 price looked extremely generous as the dark horse swept up the hill to land the spoils from future Champion Hurdle winner Granville Again. Early reports that Furlong had taken £3 million out of the ring were later scaled down to around £1 million, but in any case it was a good more than he'd had to pay to settle the little VAT difficulty.

The other prong was The Iliad, on whose Champion Hurdle bid Furlong had placed several hefty doubles with Destriero and on whom he had reportedly bet £10,000 at 33–1 with the sponsors before the gelding – SP 7–1 – had landed the Ladbroke at Leopardstown. Once Furlong had struck with Destriero in the Supreme Novices' Hurdle the potential liabilities in the ring were enormous, and as a frantic shoring up operation got under way The Iliad's price in the Champion Hurdle tumbled from an opening 12–1 to 11–2. The jitters in the ring did not last long, as The Iliad never looked like winning the Champion and trailed in last of the finishers behind Morley Street. Word was that Furlong would have cleared £10 million had The Iliad done his stuff, but no matter: his win on Destriero remains one of the great Cheltenham gambles.

Pasternak in the 1997 Cambridgeshire

Best-priced 11–1 on the morning of the race, Pasternak, trained by Sir Mark Prescott, was the subject of a major gamble, opening at 9–2 in the Newmarket betting ring before being sent off half a point shorter at 4–1. His victory over stable companion Rudimental reputedly cost the bookmakers £5 million.

Papillon in the 2000 Grand National

If there's one word guaranteed to bring a smile to the face of Channel Four Racing's Mike Cattermole it's 'Papillon' – for Mike, like so many others, was a beneficiary of one of the biggest Grand National gambles in the long history of the race when Ted Walsh's chaser held off Mely Moss in the 2000 running. For a variety of reasons Papillon, who had not been attracting abnormal business in the ante-post market during the weeks leading up to the National, became the focus of attention on the day of the race. He had been talked up in a BBC preview, and he had been picked out as an outstanding bet by the highly influential Pricewise column in the *Racing Post* on the morning of the race. From a readily available 33–1 in the early morning, Papillon opened in the on-course market at 14–1 and continued to attract shoals of money, eventually starting 10–1 joint second favourite. The rest is history.

> The longest ever starting price returned about a winner in Britain was 250–1 about Equinoctial, winner of the Grants Whisky Novices' Hurdle at Kelso on 21 November 1990. The Tote paid a comparatively skimpy dividend of £64.70 to a £1 stake – 63.7–1.

Expensive failures

Dancing Brave in the 1986 Derby

After a storming victory in the Two Thousand Guineas, Dancing Brave was the subject of a massive gamble for the Derby and went off 2–1 favourite despite doubts about his stamina. Those same doubts dictated jockey Greville Starkey's tactics, with the horse being kept in the rear of the field. Third last at Tattenham Corner, he started to make up ground in the straight, but Shahrastani had gone beyond recall, and at the post Dancing Brave was still half a length short of the lead. Burnt fingers all round.

The Fellow in the 1993 Cheltenham Gold Cup

Short-headed for steeplechasing's most prestigious prize in both 1991 and 1992, The Fellow was reportedly the most heavily backed horse in the history of the Gold Cup when going off 5–4 favourite; the recorded on-course bets alone included:

£22,000 to £16,000
£10,500 to £6,000
£7,000 to £4,000 (four times)
£6,500 to £4,000 (twice)
£12,000 to £8,000
£7,500 to £5,000
£6,000 to £4,000 (twice)

Serious stuff; but The Fellow could finish only fourth behind Jodami. Twelve months later he rewarded loyalists by winning at 7–1.

Gaelic Storm in the 1998 Stewards' Cup

The manic rush to get on Gaelic Storm for the Vodafone Stewards' Cup at Goodwood on 1 August 1998 was a prime example of the bandwagon effect – and then some.

Generally available earlier in the week at 20–1, Gaelic Storm started to attract punters' attention in the couple of days before the race as it became apparent that his trainer Mark Johnston was in top form. On the Friday – the eve of the Stewards' Cup – the wheels of the bandwagon started to turn gently, and then picked up speed considerably after the horse was recommended by one of the major telephone tipping services.

By the morning of the race Gaelic Storm had become a huge steamer – to the extent that the 16–1 still available with some firms first thing soon halved. He opened in the on-course market at 6–1 favourite before easing to a starting price of 8–1, joint market leader.

Bookmakers' liabilities were running at several million pounds by the time the stalls for the Stewards' Cup slammed open; but Gaelic Storm did not let them down, finishing fifteenth of the twenty-nine runners.

The coup

Nashwan and Pasternak are examples of bets which are often described as 'coups' – large-scale successful bets brought about by astute planning – but in both cases there was a significant bandwagon effect, with the horse's price continuing to shrink when the betting public was alerted to what was going on and rushed to get in on the action.

Often a coup will be brought about by the horse being carefully prepared for a race in such a way that the bookmakers have a less accurate idea of its chance than those who are betting on it, and will consequently let it be backed at an over-generous price; the history of the Turf is peppered with occasions when a massive amount of money invested has caused a dramatic reduction in the odds of a horse.

But the coup which pushes against – and sometimes through – the bounds of legality is easier to pull off in a small race which will attract little attention, and the most sensational frauds of the post-war era have taken place in minor events.

In April 1993 Countess Crossett – trained by Ted Caine, handler of the legendary loser Quixall Crossett – was chalked up in the ring at Kelso at 5,000–1, thought to be the longest price ever laid on a British racecourse. She started at a mere 500–1 and finished ninth of seventeen.

Francasal

A selling race at Bath on 16 July 1953 was won by a horse named Francasal at 10–1; but investigations revealed that the winner was not Francasal but a 'ringer' – a horse of similar appearance but different ability, in this case a much faster animal named Santa Amaro. The main perpetrators of the affair were convicted and jailed.

Flockton Grey

Suspicions were aroused when Flockton Grey won a two-year-old maiden race at Leicester in March 1982 at 10–1, not least because he won so easily – by twenty lengths. The horse turned out to be the three-year-old Good Hand. Again, those who had masterminded the coup ended up in court, and Flockton Grey himself spent years in police custody: he was subsequently co-owned by Michael Aspel.

Gay Future

Perhaps the most ingenious stroke of all was the Gay Future affair: planned in Ireland, prepared in Scotland, and culminating in Cumbria, at Cartmel on August Bank Holiday 1974.

The architects of the coup had sent an unnamed horse to the stables of trainer Anthony Collins at Troon in Scotland. Collins had entered a horse called Gay Future and another horse, Racionzer, in the race at Cartmel, and two other horses – Opera Cloak and Ankerwyke – in races at other courses on the same day, both starting within half an hour of the Cartmel race. On that Bank Holiday morning, 26 August, members of the syndicate who were staging the coup placed bets in a variety of betting shops in London: doubles connecting Gay

Future with Opera Cloak or with Ankerwyke. Doubles are deemed by bookmakers to be 'mugs' bets', and betting in small amounts in this manner would not have aroused suspicion.

Meanwhile the real Gay Future, who had been prepared for his race in Ireland, had been brought over the Irish Sea, swapped for the horse in Collins's charge, and sent off to Cartmel to run in the Ulverston Novices' Hurdle. Neither Ankerwyke nor Opera Cloak reached the courses where they were supposed to be running; indeed, it transpired later that they had never left their trainer's stable.

When one leg of a double is a non-runner the bet becomes a single on the remaining horse, so the failure of the other two horses to show meant that a large amount of money was now running on Gay Future; but the 'blower' system which transmits off-course money to the course betting market was not operating to Cartmel on that very busy Bank Holiday Monday (as the planners of the coup had cleverly been aware), and by the time the bookmakers – with no mobile phones in those days – realized what was afoot the only way they could get his price down was to send a representative to the course to bet on him there. The bookies' man did not arrive in time.

Before he had entered the paddock at Cartmel, Gay Future's flanks had had soap flakes rubbed into them to give the impression that he was sweating freely and so put off on-course punters, keeping the price up. The horse played his own part in the coup by strolling home fifteen lengths in front of his rivals at 10–1. Most of the betting shops who had taken the bets withheld payment, though some later regarded the matter as a legitimate coup and paid out. (The conspirators stood to win around £300,000.)

The police launched a prosecution; Collins and Tony Murphy, the Irish building contractor who was the main brain behind the coup, were convicted of conspiracy to defraud the bookmakers, and fined.

Whether or not the matter should have been brought to court was a question hotly debated at the time; whatever the legality or illegality of the episode, the Gay Future affair was certainly a coup of remarkable cunning and ingenuity.

SAYINGS OF THE BIG HITTERS

Many gallons of printers' ink have been poured into the attempt to divine the secrets of those few legendary figures who have made their betting pay in spectacular fashion. Understandably, they tend to be sparing with their guidance; but here are a few words of wisdom from three of the great backers of horses which even the humblest punter might find worth pondering.

J. P. McManus

John Patrick McManus is a legendary Irish punter and owner of many good racehorses including the great hurdler Istabraq (on which horse there was a single bet of £130,000 to win £80,000 – 13–8 on – in the Martell Aintree Hurdle on Grand National Day 1998: Istabraq was beaten a head by Pridwell). Sir Peter O'Sullevan, a close friend, memorably summed up the nature of the McManus approach to betting: 'Betting has to be intuition, not spontaneity. John knows the difference between involvement and commitment; like with a ham omelette – the chicken is involved, the pig is committed.'

This is JP's own betting philosophy:

Racing is a great leveller. The day you think you have mastered the game, you will be made to pay for it the

> *following day. What you must do is build up a bank of experience that allows you to reduce and eliminate as far as possible the factors that make for foolish betting. In a word, you act to strict ground rules always and you endeavour to become an investor rather than a pure addictive gambler.*

Barney Curley

Owner, trainer, gambler – most famously as the brains behind the Yellow Sam coup at Bellewstown in Ireland in 1975, when the single telephone in the village was commandeered by an associate, thus preventing off-course money carefully bet on the horse getting into the on-course market. 'There was this heavily built man,' according to Curley himself, 'a tough sort of guy, who suddenly discovered that a close relation of his was seriously ill and he had to keep in constant touch with the hospital. Once he had the phone in his hand he was not going to let go. He was broad enough in the beam not to permit anyone past him into the box.' Yellow Sam pulled off a major touch by winning at a starting price of 20–1 – though in running you could only get 2–1! . . .

> *Professionals never bet on the six races on the card simply for the sake of having a bet. They don't see the last race as the 'getting out' stakes, should they be behind at that point. They will bring the shutters down if their main bet of the day on one of the earlier races is a losing one and look forward to the next day or their next opportunity to apply their judgement of form and the homework they will have to put in. They know that their*

knowledge must inevitably pay off once they can control their emotions and not chase losses.

Phil Bull

When Phil Bull, founder of Timeform and one of the best brains racing has ever known, was asked for Ten Commandments to accompany an article about him in the *Daily Telegraph* magazine in 1970, he wrote two versions – one of which serves as a checklist for all punters . . .

Seek where thou wilt for winners, but bet only when thou seest value; deliver thyself from the temptation to bet in every race.

Put not thy faith in luck, nor the law of averages, nor thy trust in staking systems, for these are delusions.

Let thy stake be related to the depth of thy pocket and to what thou regardest as the true chance of the horse; that which hath the greater chance deserveth the greater stake.

Thou shalt not bet each-way in big fields, unless thou art well satisfied as to the value of the place bet.

Bet with Book or Tote according to thy judgement: thus shalt thou endeavour to get the best of both worlds.

Thou shalt not bet ante-post except upon horses that are known to be definite runners.

Beware the man who would sell thee a system; if thou knowest a profitable one, preserve it to thyself in silence.

Double and treble if thou must; but bet not upon objections, for thou hast not the evidence and the stewards know not what they do.

Let thy betting be informed by wisdom and diligence, and tempered by patience and caution, and leavened but a little with boldness.

Let thy bets be well within thy means: he that maketh his fortune in a week loseth his ducats in a day.

Amen to that!

A BETTING DICTIONARY

The peculiar language of betting adds to its mystique; like any language, it is easier to handle once you've learned a few basic terms. Here are a few of the commonest.

As well as definitions and explanations, the list below includes some of the slang terms used to describe odds, amounts of money, horses and other aspects of the betting operation: for some words and phrases the derivation is reasonably obvious, but others are more obscure.

Accumulator — A bet involving several horses, where the returns from each winning selection are staked on the next.

Across the card — Used of races run at the same time at different meetings.

Ante-post — Betting well in advance of the event. (See pages 99–102.)

Any to come — A term indicating that the whole or part of the returns of one bet are to be reinvested on another: for example, '£10 win Angelic, any to come £5 win Buttercup' involves an initial stake of £10, with the subsequent bet being struck only if there are returns from the first.

Bar	If a betting show is concluded '20–1 bar' it means that the horses not listed stand at 20–1 or longer.
Beeswax	Betting tax.
Board price	The price relayed to betting shops during the pre-race market moves and displayed there on the board: a punter can take this price and be on at those odds, regardless of starting price.
Bogey	The horse which represents the biggest liability in a bookmaker's book.
Bottle	2–1.
Burlington Bertie	100–30 (rhyming slang).
Canadian	Five selections combined as ten doubles, ten trebles, five fourfolds and one fivefold – 26 bets. (See page 86.) Also called a Super Yankee.
Carpet	3–1.
Century	£100.
Cockle	£10, or 10–1.
Double carpet	33–1.
Double net	20–1.

Double taps	15–8.
Early doors	Early-morning exchanges between punters and bookmakers.
Ear 'ole	6–4 (from the tic-tac signal).
Elef	11–1.
Elef a vier	11–4.
Enin	9–1 ('nine' spelt backwards).
Exacta	Tote bet which involves predicting the first and second in a race in the correct order.
Exes	6–1.

The odds in slang

For ease of reference, should you wish to communicate with your bookmaker in betting slang, here are the odds in slang, arranged in order:

evens	levels (variants: one to one and Scotch)
11–10	tips (variant: bits)
6–5	sais a ching
5–4	wrist (variant: hand to rouf)
11–8	up the arm
6–4	ear 'ole (variant: exes to rouf)

13–8	bits on the ear 'ole
7–4	shoulder (variant: neves to rouf)
15–8	double taps
2–1	bottle
9–4	top of the head (variant: enin to rouf)
5–2	face (variant: bottle and a half)
11–4	elef a vier
3–1	carpet (variants: tres and gimmel)
100–30	Burlington Bertie (variant: scruffy and dirty)
7–2	carpet and a half
4–1	rouf (variant: quat)
9–2	on the shoulders (variant: rouf and a half)
5–1	hand (variant: ching)
11–2	hand and a half (variant: ching and a half)
6–1	exes
13–2	exes and a half
7–1	neves
15–2	neves and a half
8–1	T.H.
9–1	enin
10–1	net (variant: cockle)
11–1	elef
12–1	net and bice
14–1	net and rouf
16–1	net and ex
20–1	score (variants: apple core and double net)
25–1	pony (variant: macaroni)
33–1	double carpet

Face	5–2 (tic-tac).
Faces	Punters in the betting ring well known to the bookmakers as being well informed.
Fiddlers	Bookmakers who will lay only small bets.
Fivefold	A five-horse accumulator.
Flimping	Giving under the odds; underpaying.
Fourfold	A four-horse accumulator.
Goliath	Bet involving 247 combinations with 8 selections in separate events: 28 doubles, 56 trebles, 70 fourfolds, 56 fivefolds, 28 sixfolds, 8 sevenfolds and one eightfold.
Grand	£1,000.
Hand	5–1 (tic-tac).
Hedging	Bookmakers reducing their liabilities by backing the horse themselves.
Heinz	Bet combining six selections in separate races in 57 bets: 15 doubles, 20 trebles, 15 fourfolds, 6 fivefolds and one sixfold.
Jolly	The favourite (the 'jolly old favourite').

Kite	Cheque.
Knock	Owe.
Levels	Evens (variant: 'levels you devils!').
Lucky 15	Bet involving four selections in 15 bets: 4 singles, 6 doubles, 4 trebles and one fourfold. (See page 86.)
Macaroni	25–1.
Monkey	£500.
Nanny	The Tote ('nanny goat').
Nap	A newspaper tipster's best bet of the day.
Nelsons	Cash (Nelson Eddies . . . readies).
Net	10–1 ('ten' spelt backwards).
Net and bice	12–1.
Net and rouf	14–1.
Net and ex	16–1.
Neves	7–1 ('seven' spelt backwards).
Not off	Said of a horse thought not to be trying to win.

On the shoulders	9–2.
Over-broke	Betting with no profit margin (see page 78 above).
Over-round	Betting with the margin in the bookie's favour (see page 76 above).
Patent	Bet involving three selections in seven bets: 3 singles, 3 doubles and one treble. (See page 84.)
Pony	£25, or 25–1.
Rag	An outsider – a horse with no apparent chance.
Rails bookmaker	One of a select group of racecourse bookmakers situated in the Tattersalls enclosure by the rail dividing that area from Members (where bookmakers are not usually allowed) – thus enabling members to bet from within their own enclosure.
Rick	Error.
Rock cake	Small bet.
Rouf	4–1 ('four' spelt backwards; pronounced 'rofe').

Rule 4	Rule governing the effect on the market of a horse's being withdrawn just before the off: see page 103.
Sais a ching	6–5.
Score	£20.
Shoulder	7–4 (tic-tac).
Skinner	A horse unbacked – if he wins the bookmakers pay out nothing.
Sky-rocket	Pocket.
Sleeper	Uncollected winnings.
Starting price	The price at which the horse is officially judged to have started the race.
Steamer	A horse gambled on significantly on the morning of the race.
Super Heinz	Bet involving seven selections in different races in 120 bets: 21 doubles, 35 trebles, 35 fourfolds, 21 fivefolds, 6 fivefolds, 7 sixfolds and one sevenfold.
Super Yankee	See *Canadian*, above.
Tank	Reserves of cash.
T.H.	8–1.

Thick 'un	A big bet.
Tic-tac	Sign language used on a racecourse by bookmakers to communicate with one another.
Tips	11–10 (tic-tac).
Tissue	The course bookmakers' forecast of how the betting will open, prepared by a form expert employed by the bookies.
Ton	£100.
Top of the head	9–4 (tic-tac).
Up the arm	11–8 (tic-tac).
Village	The whole bookmaking fraternity.
With the thumb	The price is being taken and won't last long (tic-tac).
Wrist	5–4 (tic-tac).
Yankee	Bet combining four horses in separate races in eleven bets: 6 doubles, 4 trebles and one fourfold. (See page 85.)

Ready reckoner

If you're using this, you've backed a winner. Or maybe you're working out what you would have won had the creature not fallen at the last – never a good idea. In either case, use the Ready Reckoner in this way:

Match your stake to the odds and read off the amount returned for a win bet or a place bet at one-quarter or one-fifth the odds.

Remember that the returns include your original stake, and that the figures in the Ready Reckoner do not include tax, which will be taken off your returns (not just your winnings) on off-course bets, unless you have bet 'tax paid'. Thus, 50p staked at 11–10 against returns £1.05 (55p winnings and 50p stake); 50p staked at 10–11 returns 95p (45p winnings and 50p stake). To find the return on a £1 each-way bet (a quarter the odds a place) at 6–1 you need to find the win element (£7.00) and add to it the place element (£2.50). Your returns are £9.50, of which £2 is your original stake.

Say you have a £1 double, and both horses win – at evens and 10–11. The first bet returns £2, which sum goes on to the second horse; when that one wins you end up with £3.82 – of which £1 is your original stake and £2.82 is your profit. For trebles, accumulators and more complex combination bets simply work through all the different individual stages.

Stake	Win	$^1/_5$ place return	$^1/_4$ place return

Evens

Stake	Win	$^1/_5$ place return	$^1/_4$ place return
.01	.02	.01	.01
.02	.04	.02	.02
.03	.06	.04	.04
.04	.08	.05	.05
.05	.10	.06	.06
.10	.20	.12	.12
.20	.40	.24	.25
.30	.60	.36	.37
.40	.80	.48	.50
.50	1.00	.60	.62
1.00	2.00	1.20	1.25
2.00	4.00	2.40	2.50
5.00	10.00	6.00	6.25

Win	1/5 place return	1/4 place return	Stake	Win	1/5 place return	1/4 place return
11–10 against						**11–10 on**
.02	.01	.01	.01	.02	.01	.01
.04	.02	.02	.02	.04	.02	.02
.06	.04	.04	.03	.06	.04	.04
.08	.05	.05	.04	.08	.05	.05
.10	.06	.06	.05	.10	.06	.06
.21	.12	.13	.10	.19	.12	.12
.42	.24	.25	.20	.38	.24	.25
.63	.37	.38	.30	.57	.35	.37
.84	.49	.51	.40	.76	.47	.49
1.05	.61	.64	.50	.95	.59	.62
2.10	1.22	1.27	1.00	1.91	1.18	1.23
4.20	2.44	2.55	2.00	3.82	2.36	2.46
10.50	6.10	5.37	5.00	9.55	5.91	6.15

Win	1/5 place return	1/4 place return	Stake	Win	1/5 place return	1/4 place return
6–5 against						**6–5 on**
.02	.01	.01	.01	.02	.01	.01
.04	.02	.03	.02	.04	.02	.02
.07	.04	.04	.03	.05	.03	.04
.09	.05	.05	.04	.07	.05	.05
.11	.06	.06	.05	.09	.06	.06
.22	.12	.13	.10	.18	.12	.12
.44	.25	.26	.20	.37	.23	.24
.66	.37	.39	.30	.55	.35	.36
.88	.50	.52	.40	.73	.46	.48
1.10	.62	.65	.50	.92	.58	.60
2.20	1.24	1.30	1.00	1.83	1.17	1.21
4.40	2.48	2.60	2.00	3.67	2.33	2.42
11.00	6.20	6.50	5.00	9.17	5.83	6.05

Win	1/5 place return	1/4 place return	Stake	Win	1/5 place return	1/4 place return
5–4 against						**5–4 on**
.02	.01	.01	.01	.02	.01	.01
.04	.02	.03	.02	.04	.02	.02
.07	.04	.04	.03	.05	.03	.04
.09	.05	.05	.04	.07	.05	.05
.11	.06	.07	.05	.09	.06	.06
.22	.12	.13	.10	.18	.12	.12
.45	.25	.26	.20	.36	.23	.24
.67	.37	.39	.30	.54	.35	.36
.90	.50	.52	.40	.72	.46	.48
1.12	.62	.66	.50	.90	.58	.60
2.25	1.25	1.31	1.00	1.80	1.16	1.20
4.50	2.50	2.62	2.00	3.60	2.32	2.40
11.25	6.25	6.56	5.00	9.00	5.80	6.00

Win	1/5 place return	1/4 place return	Stake	Win	1/5 place return	1/4 place return
11–8 against						**11–8 on**
.02	.01	.01	.01	.02	.01	.01
.05	.03	.03	.02	.03	.02	.02
.07	.04	.04	.03	.05	.03	.04
.09	.05	.05	.04	.07	.05	.05
.12	.06	.07	.05	.09	.06	.06
.24	.13	.13	.10	.17	.11	.12
.47	.25	.27	.20	.35	.23	.24
.71	.38	.40	.30	.52	.34	.35
.95	.51	.54	.40	.69	.46	.47
1.19	.64	.67	.50	.86	.57	.59
2.37	1.27	1.34	1.00	1.73	1.15	1.18
4.75	2.55	2.68	2.00	3.45	2.29	2.36
11.87	6.37	6.71	5.00	8.64	5.73	5.91

Win	1/5 place return	1/4 place return	Stake	Win	1/5 place return	1/4 place return
6–4 against						**6–4 on**
.02	.01	.01	.01	.02	.01	.01
.05	.03	.03	.02	.03	.02	.02
.07	.04	.04	.03	.05	.03	.04
.10	.05	.05	.04	.07	.05	.05
.12	.06	.07	.05	.08	.06	.06
.25	.13	.14	.10	.17	.11	.12
.50	.26	.27	.20	.33	.23	.23
.75	.39	.41	.30	.50	.34	.35
1.00	.52	.55	.40	.67	.45	.47
1.25	.65	.69	.50	.83	.57	.58
2.50	1.30	1.37	1.00	1.66	1.13	1.17
5.00	2.60	2.75	2.00	3.33	2.27	2.33
12.50	6.50	6.87	5.00	8.33	5.67	5.83

Win	1/5 place return	1/4 place return	Stake	Win	1/5 place return	1/4 place return
13–8 against						**13–8 on**
.03	.01	.01	.01	.02	.01	.01
.05	.03	.03	.02	.03	.02	.02
.08	.04	.04	.03	.05	.03	.03
.10	.05	.06	.04	.06	.04	.05
.13	.07	.07	.05	.08	.06	.06
.26	.13	.14	.10	.16	.11	.12
.52	.26	.28	.20	.32	.22	.23
.79	.40	.42	.30	.48	.34	.35
1.05	.53	.56	.40	.65	.45	.46
1.31	.66	.70	.50	.81	.56	.58
2.62	1.32	1.40	1.00	1.62	1.11	1.15
5.25	2.65	2.81	2.00	3.23	2.25	2.31
13.12	6.62	7.03	5.00	8.08	5.62	5.77

Win	1/5 place return	1/4 place return	Stake	Win	1/5 place return	1/4 place return
7–4 against						**7–4 on**
.03	.01	.01	.01	.02	.01	.01
.05	.03	.03	.02	.03	.02	.02
.08	.04	.04	.03	.05	.03	.03
.11	.05	.06	.04	.06	.04	.05
.14	.07	.07	.05	.08	.06	.06
.27	.13	.14	.10	.16	.11	.11
.55	.27	.29	.20	.32	.22	.23
.82	.40	.43	.30	.47	.33	.34
1.10	.54	.57	.40	.63	.45	.46
1.37	.67	.72	.50	.79	.56	.57
2.75	1.35	1.44	1.00	1.57	1.11	1.14
5.50	2.70	2.87	2.00	3.14	2.23	2.28
13.75	6.75	7.19	5.00	7.86	5.57	5.71

Win	1/5 place return	1/4 place return	Stake	Win	1/5 place return	1/4 place return
15–8 against						**15–8 on**
.03	.01	.01	.01	.02	.01	.01
.06	.03	.03	.02	.03	.02	.02
.09	.04	.04	.03	.05	.03	.03
.11	.05	.06	.04	.06	.04	.05
.14	.07	.07	.05	.08	.06	.06
.29	.13	.14	.10	.15	.11	.11
.57	.27	.29	.20	.31	.22	.23
.86	.41	.44	.30	.46	.33	.34
1.15	.55	.59	.40	.61	.44	.45
1.44	.69	.73	.50	.77	.55	.57
2.87	1.37	1.47	1.00	1.53	1.11	1.13
5.75	2.75	2.94	2.00	3.07	2.21	2.26
14.37	6.87	7.34	5.00	7.67	5.53	5.67

Win	1/5 place return	1/4 place return	Stake	Win	1/5 place return	1/4 place return
2–1 against						**2–1 on**
.03	.01	.01	.01	.01	.01	.01
.06	.03	.03	.02	.03	.02	.02
.09	.04	.04	.03	.04	.03	.03
.12	.06	.06	.04	.06	.04	.05
.15	.07	.07	.05	.07	.05	.06
.30	.14	.15	.10	.15	.11	.11
.60	.28	.30	.20	.30	.22	.23
.90	.42	.45	.30	.45	.33	.34
1.20	.56	.60	.40	.60	.44	.45
1.50	.70	.75	.50	.75	.55	.56
3.00	1.40	1.50	1.00	1.50	1.10	1.13
6.00	2.80	3.00	2.00	3.00	2.20	2.25
15.00	7.00	7.50	5.00	7.50	5.50	5.63

Win	1/5 place return	1/4 place return	Stake	Win	1/5 place return	1/4 place return
9–4 against						**9–4 on**
.03	.01	.02	.01	.01	.01	.02
.06	.03	.03	.02	.03	.02	.02
.10	.04	.05	.03	.04	.03	.03
.13	.06	.06	.04	.06	.04	.04
.16	.07	.08	.05	.07	.05	.06
.32	.14	.16	.10	.14	.11	.11
.65	.29	.31	.20	.29	.22	.22
.97	.43	.47	.30	.43	.33	.33
1.30	.58	.62	.40	.58	.44	.44
1.62	.72	.78	.50	.72	.54	.56
3.25	1.45	1.56	1.00	1.44	1.09	1.11
6.50	2.90	3.11	2.00	2.89	2.18	2.22
16.25	7.25	7.81	5.00	7.22	5.44	5.56

Win	1/5 place return	1/4 place return	Stake	Win	1/5 place return	1/4 place return
5–2 against						**5–2 on**
.03	.01	.02	.01	.01	.01	.01
.07	.03	.03	.02	.03	.02	.02
.10	.04	.05	.03	.04	.03	.03
.14	.06	.06	.04	.06	.04	.04
.17	.07	.08	.05	.07	.05	.05
.35	.15	.16	.10	.14	.11	.11
.70	.30	.32	.20	.28	.22	.22
1.05	.45	.49	.30	.42	.32	.33
1.40	.60	.65	.40	.56	.43	.44
1.75	.75	.81	.50	.70	.54	.55
3.50	1.50	1.62	1.00	1.40	1.08	1.10
7.00	3.00	3.25	2.00	2.80	2.16	2.20
17.50	7.50	8.12	5.00	7.00	5.40	5.50

Win	1/5 place return	1/4 place return	Stake	Win	1/5 place return	1/4 place return
11–4 against						**11–4 on**
.04	.02	.02	.01	.01	.01	.01
.07	.03	.03	.02	.03	.02	.02
.11	.05	.05	.03	.04	.03	.03
.15	.06	.07	.04	.05	.04	.04
.19	.08	.08	.05	.07	.05	.05
.37	.16	.17	.10	.14	.11	.11
.75	.31	.34	.20	.27	.21	.22
1.12	.46	.51	.30	.41	.32	.33
1.50	.62	.67	.40	.55	.43	.44
1.87	.77	.84	.50	.68	.54	.55
3.75	1.55	1.69	1.00	1.36	1.07	1.08
7.50	3.10	3.37	2.00	2.73	2.14	2.18
18.75	7.75	8.44	5.00	6.82	5.36	5.45

Win	1/5 place return	1/4 place return	Stake	Win	1/5 place return	1/4 place return
3–1 against						**3–1 on**
.04	.02	.02	.01	.01	.01	.01
.08	.03	.04	.02	.03	.02	.02
.12	.05	.05	.03	.04	.03	.03
.16	.06	.07	.04	.05	.04	.04
.20	.08	.09	.05	.07	.05	.05
.40	.16	.17	.10	.13	.11	.11
.80	.32	.35	.20	.27	.21	.22
1.20	.48	.52	.30	.40	.32	.33
1.60	.64	.70	.40	.53	.43	.43
2.00	.80	.87	.50	.67	.53	.54
4.00	1.60	1.75	1.00	1.33	1.07	1.08
8.00	3.20	3.50	2.00	2.67	2.13	2.17
20.00	8.00	8.75	5.00	6.67	5.33	5.42

Win	1/5 place return	1/4 place return	Stake	Win	1/5 place return	1/4 place return
100–30 against				**7–2 against**		
.04	.02	.02	.01	.04	.02	.02
.09	.03	.04	.02	.09	.03	.04
.13	.05	.05	.03	.13	.05	.06
.17	.07	.07	.04	.18	.07	.07
.22	.08	.09	.05	.22	.08	.09
.43	.17	.18	.10	.45	.17	.19
.87	.33	.37	.20	.90	.34	.37
1.30	.50	.55	.30	1.35	.51	.56
1.73	.67	.73	.40	1.80	.68	.75
2.17	.83	.92	.50	2.25	.85	.94
4.33	1.67	1.83	1.00	4.50	1.70	1.87
8.67	3.33	3.67	2.00	9.00	3.40	3.75
21.67	8.33	9.17	5.00	22.50	8.50	9.37

Win	1/5 place return	1/4 place return	Stake	Win	1/5 place return	1/4 place return
4–1 against						**9–2 against**
.05	.02	.02	.01	.05	.02	.02
.10	.04	.04	.02	.11	.04	.04
.15	.05	.06	.03	.16	.06	.06
.20	.07	.08	.04	.22	.08	.08
.25	.09	.10	.05	.27	.09	.11
.50	.18	.20	.10	.55	.19	.21
1.00	.36	.40	.20	1.10	.38	.42
1.50	.54	.60	.30	1.65	.57	.64
2.00	.72	.80	.40	2.20	.76	.85
2.50	.90	1.00	.50	2.75	.95	1.06
5.00	1.80	2.00	1.00	5.50	1.90	2.12
10.00	3.60	4.00	2.00	11.00	3.80	4.25
25.00	9.00	10.00	5.00	27.50	9.50	10.62

Win	$^1/_5$ place return	$^1/_4$ place return	Stake	Win	$^1/_5$ place return	$^1/_4$ place return
5–1 against						**11–2 against**
.06	.02	.02	.01	.06	.02	.02
.12	.04	.04	.02	.13	.04	.05
.18	.06	.07	.03	.19	.06	.07
.24	.08	.09	.04	.26	.08	.09
.30	.10	.11	.05	.32	.10	.12
.60	.20	.22	.10	.65	.21	.24
1.20	.40	.45	.20	1.30	.42	.48
1.80	.60	.67	.30	1.95	.63	.71
2.40	.80	.90	.40	2.60	.84	.95
3.00	1.00	1.12	.50	3.25	1.05	1.19
6.00	2.00	2.25	1.00	6.50	2.10	2.38
12.00	4.00	4.50	2.00	13.00	4.20	4.75
30.00	10.00	11.25	5.00	32.50	10.50	11.87

Win	1/5 place return	1/4 place return	Stake	Win	1/5 place return	1/4 place return
6–1 against						**13–2 against**
.07	.02	.02	.01	.07	.02	.03
.14	.04	.05	.02	.15	.05	.05
.21	.07	.07	.03	.22	.07	.08
.28	.09	.10	.04	.30	.09	.10
.35	.11	.12	.05	.37	.11	.13
.70	.22	.25	.10	.75	.23	.26
1.40	.44	.50	.20	1.50	.46	.52
2.10	.66	.75	.30	2.25	.69	.79
2.80	.88	1.00	.40	3.00	.92	1.05
3.50	1.10	1.25	.50	3.75	1.15	1.31
7.00	2.20	2.50	1.00	7.50	2.30	2.26
14.00	4.40	5.00	2.00	15.00	4.60	5.25
35.00	11.00	12.50	5.00	37.50	11.50	13.12

Win	1/5 place return	1/4 place return	Stake	Win	1/5 place return	1/4 place return
7–1 against						**15–2 against**
.08	.02	.03	.01	.08	.02	.03
.16	.05	.05	.02	.17	.05	.06
.24	.07	.08	.03	.25	.07	.09
.32	.10	.11	.04	.34	.10	.11
.40	.12	.14	.05	.42	.12	.14
.80	.24	.27	.10	.85	.25	.29
1.60	.48	.55	.20	1.70	.50	.57
2.40	.72	.82	.30	2.55	.75	.86
3.20	.96	1.10	.40	3.40	1.00	1.15
4.00	1.20	1.37	.50	4.25	1.25	1.44
8.00	2.40	2.75	1.00	8.50	2.50	2.87
16.00	4.80	5.50	2.00	17.00	5.00	5.75
40.00	12.00	13.75	5.00	42.50	12.50	14.37

Win	1/5 place return	1/4 place return	Stake	Win	1/5 place return	1/4 place return
8–1 against				**9–1 against**		
.09	.03	.03	.01	.10	.03	.03
.18	.05	.06	.02	.20	.06	.06
.27	.08	.09	.03	.30	.08	.10
.36	.10	.12	.04	.40	.11	.13
.45	.13	.15	.05	.50	.14	.16
.90	.26	.30	.10	1.00	.28	.32
1.80	.52	.60	.20	2.00	.56	.65
2.70	.78	.90	.30	3.00	.84	.97
3.60	1.04	1.20	.40	4.00	1.12	1.30
4.50	1.30	1.50	.50	5.00	1.40	1.62
9.00	2.60	3.00	1.00	10.00	2.80	3.25
18.00	5.20	6.00	2.00	20.00	5.60	6.50
45.00	13.00	15.00	5.00	50.00	14.00	16.25

Win	1/5 place return	1/4 place return	Stake	Win	1/5 place return	1/4 place return
10–1 against				**11–1 against**		
.11	.03	.03	.01	.12	.03	.04
.22	.06	.07	.02	.24	.06	.07
.33	.09	.10	.03	.36	.10	.11
.44	.12	.14	.04	.48	.13	.15
.55	.15	.17	.05	.60	.16	.19
1.10	.30	.35	.10	1.20	.32	.37
2.20	.60	.70	.20	2.40	.64	.75
3.30	.90	1.05	.30	3.60	.96	1.12
4.40	1.20	1.40	.40	4.80	1.28	1.50
5.50	1.50	1.75	.50	6.00	1.60	1.87
11.00	3.00	3.50	1.00	12.00	3.20	3.75
22.00	6.00	7.00	2.00	24.00	6.40	7.50
55.00	15.00	17.50	5.00	60.00	16.00	18.75

Win	1/5 place return	1/4 place return	Stake	Win	1/5 place return	1/4 place return
12–1 against						**14–1 against**
.13	.03	.04	.01	.15	.04	.04
.26	.07	.08	.02	.30	.08	.09
.39	.10	.12	.03	.45	.11	.13
.52	.14	.16	.04	.60	.15	.18
.65	.17	.20	.05	.75	.19	.22
1.30	.34	.40	.10	1.50	.38	.45
2.60	.68	.80	.20	3.00	.76	.90
3.90	1.02	1.20	.30	4.50	1.14	1.35
5.20	1.36	1.60	.40	6.00	1.52	1.80
6.50	1.70	2.00	.50	7.50	1.90	2.25
13.00	3.40	4.00	1.00	15.00	3.80	4.50
26.00	6.80	8.00	2.00	30.00	7.60	9.00
65.00	17.00	20.00	5.00	75.00	19.00	22.50

Win	1/5 place return	1/4 place return	Stake	Win	1/5 place return	1/4 place return
16–1 against						**20–1 against**
.17	.04	.05	.01	.21	.05	.06
.34	.08	.10	.02	.42	.10	.12
.51	.13	.15	.03	.63	.15	.18
.68	.17	.20	.04	.84	.20	.24
.85	.21	.25	.05	1.05	.25	.30
1.70	.42	.50	.10	2.10	.50	.60
3.40	.84	1.00	.20	4.20	1.00	1.20
5.10	1.26	1.50	.30	6.30	1.50	1.80
6.80	1.68	2.00	.40	8.40	2.00	2.40
8.50	2.10	2.50	.50	10.50	2.50	3.00
17.00	4.20	5.00	1.00	21.00	5.00	6.00
34.00	8.40	10.00	2.00	42.00	10.00	12.00
85.00	21.00	25.00	5.00	105.00	25.00	30.00

Win	1/5 place return	1/4 place return	Stake	Win	1/5 place return	1/4 place return
25–1 against						**33–1 against**
.26	.06	.07	.01	.34	.08	.09
.52	.12	.14	.02	.68	.15	.18
.78	.18	.22	.03	1.02	.23	.28
1.04	.24	.29	.04	1.36	.30	.37
1.30	.30	.36	.05	1.70	.38	.46
2.60	.60	.72	.10	3.40	.76	.92
5.20	1.20	1.45	.20	6.80	1.52	1.85
7.80	1.80	2.17	.30	10.20	2.28	2.77
10.40	2.40	2.90	.40	13.60	3.04	3.70
13.00	3.00	3.62	.50	17.00	3.80	4.62
26.00	6.00	7.25	1.00	34.00	7.60	9.25
52.00	12.00	14.50	2.00	68.00	15.20	18.50
130.00	30.00	36.25	5.00	170.00	38.00	46.25

Win	1/5 place return	1/4 place return	Stake	Win	1/5 place return	1/4 place return
50–1 against						**66–1 against**
.51	.11	.14	.01	.67	.14	.18
1.02	.22	.27	.02	1.34	.28	.35
1.53	.33	.41	.03	2.01	.43	.53
2.04	.44	.54	.04	2.68	.57	.70
2.55	.55	.68	.05	3.35	.71	.88
5.10	1.10	1.35	.10	6.70	1.42	1.75
10.20	2.20	2.70	.20	13.40	2.84	3.50
15.30	3.30	4.05	.30	20.10	4.26	5.25
20.40	4.40	5.40	.40	26.80	5.68	7.00
25.50	5.50	6.75	.50	33.50	7.10	8.75
51.00	11.00	13.50	1.00	67.00	14.20	17.50
102.00	22.00	27.00	2.00	134.00	28.40	35.00
255.00	55.00	67.50	5.00	335.00	71.00	87.50

100–1 against

Stake	Win	1/5 place return	1/4 place return
.01	1.01	.21	.26
.02	2.02	.42	.52
.03	3.03	.63	.78
.04	4.04	.84	1.04
.05	5.05	1.05	1.30
.10	10.10	2.10	2.60
.20	20.20	4.20	5.20
.30	30.30	6.30	7.80
.40	40.40	8.40	10.40
.50	50.50	10.50	13.00
1.00	101.00	21.00	26.00
2.00	202.00	42.00	52.00
5.00	505.00	105.00	130.00

Flat weight-for-age scale

The scale shows the number of pounds by which it is deemed the average horse in each age group falls short of maturity at different dates and distances.

Dist.	Age	Jan.		Feb.		March		April		May	
(flgs)		1–15	16–31	1–14	15–29	1–15	16–31	1–15	16–30	1–15	16–31
5	2	–	–	–	–	–	47	44	41	38	36
	3	15	15	14	14	13	12	11	10	9	8
6	2	–	–	–	–	–	–	–	–	44	41
	3	16	16	15	15	14	13	12	11	10	9
7	2	–	–	–	–	–	–	–	–	–	–
	3	18	18	17	17	16	15	14	13	12	11
8	2	–	–	–	–	–	–	–	–	–	–
	3	20	20	19	19	18	17	15	14	13	12
9	3	22	22	21	21	20	19	17	15	14	13
	4	1	1	–	–	–	–	–	–	–	–
10	3	23	23	22	22	21	20	19	17	15	14
	4	2	2	1	1	–	–	–	–	–	–
11	3	24	24	23	23	22	21	20	19	17	15
	4	3	3	2	2	1	1	–	–	–	–
12	3	25	25	24	24	23	22	21	20	19	17
	4	4	4	3	3	2	2	1	1	–	–
13	3	26	26	25	25	24	23	22	21	20	19
	4	5	5	4	4	3	3	2	1	–	–
14	3	27	27	26	26	25	24	23	22	21	20
	4	6	6	5	5	4	4	3	2	1	–
15	3	28	28	27	27	26	25	24	23	22	21
	4	6	6	5	5	4	4	3	3	2	1
16	3	29	29	28	28	27	26	25	24	23	22
	4	7	7	6	6	5	5	4	4	3	2
18	3	31	31	30	30	29	28	27	26	25	24
	4	8	8	7	7	6	6	5	5	4	3
20	3	33	33	32	32	31	30	29	28	27	26
	4	9	9	8	8	7	7	6	6	5	4

June		July		Aug.		Sept.		Oct.		Nov.		Dec.	
1–15	16–30	1–15	16–31	1–15	16–31	1–15	16–30	1–15	16–31	1–15	16–30	1–15	16–31
34	32	30	28	26	24	22	20	19	18	17	17	16	16
7	6	5	4	3	2	1	1	–	–	–	–	–	–
38	36	33	31	28	26	24	22	21	20	19	18	17	17
8	7	6	5	4	3	2	2	2	1	1	–	–	–
–	–	38	35	32	30	27	25	23	22	21	20	19	19
10	9	8	7	6	5	4	3	2	2	1	1	–	–
–	–	–	–	37	34	31	28	26	24	23	22	21	20
11	10	9	8	7	6	5	4	3	3	2	2	1	1
12	11	10	9	8	7	6	5	4	4	3	3	2	2
–	–	–	–	–	–	–	–	–	–	–	–	–	
13	12	11	10	9	8	7	6	5	5	4	4	3	3
–	–	–	–	–	–	–	–	–	–	–	–	–	–
14	13	12	11	10	9	8	7	6	6	5	5	4	4
–	–	–	–	–	–	–	–	–	–	–	–	–	–
15	14	13	12	11	10	9	8	7	7	6	6	5	5
–	–	–	–	–	–	–	–	–	–	–	–	–	–
17	15	14	13	12	11	10	9	8	8	7	7	6	6
–	–	–	–	–	–	–	–	–	–	–	–	–	–
19	17	15	14	13	12	11	10	9	9	8	8	7	7
–	–	–	–	–	–	–	–	–	–	–	–	–	–
20	19	17	15	14	13	12	11	10	9	8	8	7	7
–	–	–	–	–	–	–	–	–	–	–	–	–	–
21	20	19	17	15	14	13	12	11	10	9	9	8	8
1	–	–	–	–	–	–	–	–	–	–	–	–	–
23	22	21	20	18	16	14	13	12	11	10	10	9	9
2	1	–	–	–	–	–	–	–	–	–	–	–	–
25	24	23	22	20	18	16	14	13	12	11	11	10	10
3	2	1	–	–	–	–	–	–	–	–	–	–	–

Jumping weight-for-age scale

The scale shows the weight allowances, in pounds, which three-year-olds and four-year-olds will receive from horses aged five and upwards in hurdle races, and which four-year-olds and five-year-olds will receive from horses aged six and upwards in steeplechases. (Minute changes to this scale came into effect in 1999, but for simplicity's sake we are presenting it in its basic form.)

Hurdle races

Dist. (m)	Age	Jan.	Feb.	March	April	May	June
2	3	–	–	–	–	–	–
	4	12	10	8	6	5	5
$2^1/_2$	3	–	–	–	–	–	–
	4	13	11	9	7	6	6
3	3	–	–	–	–	–	–
	4	14	12	10	8	7	7

Steeplechases

Dist. (m)	Age	Jan.	Feb.	March	April	May	June
2	4	–	–	–	–	–	–
	5	10	9	8	7	6	6
$2^1/_2$	4	–	–	–	–	–	–
	5	11	10	9	8	7	7
3	4	–	–	–	–	–	–
	5	12	11	10	9	8	8

July	Aug.	Sept.	Oct.	Nov.	Dec.
20	20	18	17	16	14
3	3	2	1	–	–
21	21	19	18	17	15
3	3	2	1	–	–
23	23	21	19	18	16
4	4	3	2	1	–

July	Aug.	Sept.	Oct.	Nov.	Dec.
15	15	14	13	12	11
3	3	2	1	–	–
16	16	15	14	13	12
4	4	3	2	1	–
17	17	16	15	14	13
5	5	4	3	2	1

Leading trainers course by course

Knowing which trainers send out significant numbers of winners on particular courses can be a very effective way of pinpointing horses to back – especially when a lesser known trainer is high up the ranking. The list below gives for each course the top Flat trainers 1995–2000 and top jumps trainers from 1995 to the end of the 1999–2000 season.

	winners	*runners*	*strike rate (%)*
Aintree			
M. Pipe	22	140	16
N. Twiston-Davies	11	83	13
P. Hobbs	9	64	14
P. Nicholls	8	45	18
Howard Johnson	8	38	21
Ascot			
Flat			
Saeed bin Suroor	28	120	23
J. Gosden	26	155	17
Sir Michael Stoute	22	163	13
R. Hannon	19	208	9
M. Johnston	18	136	13
jumps			
M. Pipe	26	127	21
N. Twiston-Davies	18	117	15
N. Henderson	17	126	14
K. Bailey	15	68	22
J. Gifford	14	139	10
Ayr			
Flat			
B. Hills	26	86	30
M. Johnston	23	180	13

Miss L. Perratt	18	286	6
J. Goldie	14	217	6
J Dunlop	11	44	25
jumps			
L. Lungo	39	250	16
Mrs M. Reveley	34	180	19
P. Monteith	21	157	13
J. Goldie	20	146	14
C. Parker	19	115	17

Bangor-on-Dee

M. Pipe	39	159	25
N. Twiston-Davies	28	118	24
Mrs S. Smith	13	139	9
P. Hobbs	11	45	24
J. J. O'Neill	10	76	13

Bath

M. Channon	20	149	13
I. Balding	19	108	18
B. Hills	14	94	15
R. Hannon	14	139	10
J. Hills	13	81	16

Beverley

T. Easterby	34	288	12
M. Johnston	28	155	18
M. Easterby	16	227	7
J. Dunlop	14	52	27
Mrs M. Reveley	14	79	18

Brighton

R. Hannon	41	259	16
G. L. Moore	34	295	12
M. Channon	20	142	14
K. Ivory	16	89	18
Miss G. Kelleway	16	105	15

Carlisle

Flat			
M. Johnston	15	79	19
J. L. Eyre	12	74	16
E. Alston	9	78	12
Mrs M. Reveley	7	44	16
D. Nicholls	7	78	9
jumps			
Mrs M. Reveley	37	138	27
L. Lungo	28	180	16
J. J. O'Neill	18	155	12
Mrs S. Smith	16	127	13
C. Parker	16	137	12

Cartmel

M. Pipe	12	24	50
P. Bowen	11	24	46
G. M. Moore	10	28	36
Mrs S. Smith	10	56	18
M. C. Chapman	8	77	10

Catterick

Flat			
D. Nicholls	22	147	15
Mrs M. Reveley	19	102	19
M. W. Easterby	19	172	11
B. Hills	18	60	30
T. Easterby	17	135	13
jumps			
Mrs M. Reveley	37	172	22
Mrs S. Smith	21	149	14
M. Hammond	18	180	10
T. Easterby	16	80	20
M. W. Easterby	14	101	14

Cheltenham

M. Pipe	67	455	15

N. Twiston-Davies	27	275	10
N. Henderson	24	162	15
Miss V. Williams	18	78	23
P. Hobbs	15	168	9

Chepstow

Flat			
R. Hannon	14	124	11
J. M. Bradley	13	161	8
L. Cumani	11	28	39
J. Dunlop	10	52	19
Sir Michael Stoute	9	30	30
jumps			
M. Pipe	57	271	21
P. Hobbs	39	153	26
P. Nicholls	39	146	27
N. Twiston-Davies	22	163	14
Miss V. Williams	12	36	33

Chester

B. Hills	18	108	17
P. D. Evans	17	196	9
A. Bailey	15	142	11
E. Alston	14	145	10
J. Dunlop	12	38	32

Doncaster

Flat			
B. Hills	53	276	19
J. Dunlop	35	175	20
J. Gosden	31	164	19
H. Cecil	29	127	23
Saeed bin Suroor	20	55	36
jumps			
Mrs M. Reveley	22	134	16
N. Henderson	14	41	34
T. Easterby	12	49	25

Mrs S. Smith	10	56	18
Miss H. Knight	10	36	28

Epsom Downs

R. Hannon	17	139	12
M. Johnston	14	67	21
P. Cole	11	57	19
I. Balding	11	83	13
H. Cecil	9	37	24

Exeter

M. Pipe	83	363	23
P. Hobbs	65	236	28
Miss H. Knight	36	174	21
R. Frost	36	250	14
N. Twiston-Davies	17	107	16

Fakenham

O. Brennan	13	42	31
Miss D. Haine	9	47	19
N. Henderson	6	14	43
Mrs P. Sly	6	25	24
S. Gollings	5	20	25

Folkestone

Flat			
R. Hannon	14	111	13
S. C. Williams	12	51	24
J. Dunlop	9	48	19
P. Cole	8	43	19
Miss G. Kelleway	8	59	14
jumps			
D. M. Grissell	18	92	20
M. Pipe	17	50	34
N. Henderson	17	39	44
J. Gifford	12	100	12
Miss V. Williams	10	18	56

Fontwell Park

M. Pipe	38	167	23
P. Nicholls	36	91	40
J. Gifford	26	182	14
P. Hobbs	21	86	24
Miss V. Williams	20	45	44

Goodwood

J. Gosden	40	167	24
R. Hannon	33	356	9
P. Cole	28	136	21
Sir Michael Stoute	27	113	24
H. Cecil	26	105	25

Hamilton Park

M. Johnston	35	177	20
Miss L. Perratt	35	372	9
M.Channon	15	55	27
J. Goldie	15	212	7
D. Haydn Jones	14	66	21

Haydock Park

Flat			
J. Dunlop	31	122	25
J. Gosden	22	108	20
B. Hills	19	109	17
H. Cecil	17	46	37
T. Easterby	17	160	11
jumps			
M. Pipe	45	189	24
N. Twiston-Davies	18	112	16
Mrs M. Reveley	15	86	17
Miss V. Williams	12	32	38
J. M. Jefferson	12	43	28

Hereford

M. Pipe	42	149	28
N. Twiston-Davies	35	176	20
P. Hobbs	17	112	15
Miss V. Williams	16	49	33
K. Bailey	15	91	17

Hexham

L. Lungo	30	143	21
G. M. Moore	22	119	19
Mrs S. Smith	16	153	11
M. Hammond	16	126	13
Howard Johnson	12	119	10

Huntingdon

K. Bailey	25	137	18
Mrs M. Reveley	21	81	26
N. Henderson	15	61	25
M. Pipe	12	53	23
J. Gifford	12	105	11

Kelso

Mrs M. Reveley	39	162	24
M.Hammond	30	158	19
L. Lungo	19	120	16
J. J. O'Neill	15	63	24
P. Montieth	14	157	9

Kempton Park

Flat			
R. Hannon	28	260	11
Sir Michael Stoute	18	93	19
J. Dunlop	17	109	16
H. Cecil	16	61	26
D. Elsworth	14	101	14
jumps			
N. Henderson	24	112	21
P. Nicholls	15	50	30

R. Alner	15	52	29
M. Pipe	14	83	17
N. Twiston-Davies	13	77	17

Leicester

Flat

R. Hannon	28	179	16
J. Dunlop	27	157	17
Sir Michael Stoute	20	78	26
B. Hills	16	79	20
P. Cole	16	107	15

jumps

M. Pipe	28	97	29
N. Henderson	14	42	33
Miss H. Knight	10	48	21
N. Twiston-Davies	8	45	18
Miss V. Williams	6	25	24

Lingfield Park

Flat (turf)

R. Hannon	28	232	12
J. Dunlop	24	124	19
H. Cecil	18	46	39
Sir Michael Stoute	16	72	22
B. Meehan	13	89	15

Flat (all-weather)

G. L. Moore	101	687	15
M. Johnston	47	228	21
K. Burke	42	286	15
Miss G. Kelleway	42	331	13
R. Hannon	41	263	16

jumps

M. Pipe	20	63	32
G. L. Moore	13	60	22
J. Gifford	9	43	21
N. Twiston-Davies	9	41	22
A. Turnell	6	33	18

Ludlow

M. Pipe	43	143	30
K. Bailey	26	122	21
N. Twiston-Davies	17	138	12
N. Henderson	16	39	41
P. Nicholls	15	49	31

Market Rasen

Mrs M. Reveley	44	173	25
M. Pipe	30	121	25
Mrs S. Smith	22	154	14
M. C. Chapman	18	304	6
Miss H. Knight	15	46	33

Musselburgh

Flat			
M. Johnston	20	115	17
J. Goldie	20	194	10
Mrs M. Reveley	16	114	14
M. Easterby	12	52	23
M. Bell	11	28	39
jumps			
Howard Johnson	29	149	20
M. Hammond	23	169	13
P. Monteith	19	125	15
F. Murphy	15	56	27
L. Lungo	15	72	21

Newbury

Flat			
J. Gosden	28	143	20
J. Dunlop	28	189	15
R. Hannon	22	419	5
H. Cecil	21	103	20
P. Cole	20	146	14
jumps			
M. Pipe	28	135	21

N. Henderson	26	143	18
N. Twiston-Davies	22	136	16
P. Nicholls	12	62	19
O. Sherwood	12	59	20

Newcastle

Flat			
M. Johnston	36	214	17
T. Easterby	18	188	10
J. Dunlop	16	63	25
H. Cecil	13	27	48
M. Bell	13	50	26
jumps			
Mrs M. Reveley	62	246	25
M. Easterby	26	136	19
L. Lungo	20	138	15
J. M. Jefferson	18	80	23
M. Hammond	15	153	10

Newmarket

Flat: Rowley Mile			
H. Cecil	41	175	23
Saeed bin Suroor	23	88	26
B. Hills	23	279	8
Sir Michael Stoute	20	194	10
R. Hannon	20	271	7
Flat: July Course			
J. Gosden	38	186	20
J. Dunlop	33	214	15
H. Cecil	31	139	22
R. Hannon	26	284	9
L. Cumani	24	151	16

Newton Abbot

M. Pipe	105	425	25
P. Hobbs	61	236	26
P. Nicholls	37	166	22

R. Frost	36	325	11
K. Bailey	16	55	29

Nottingham

J. Dunlop	25	149	17
H. Cecil	18	61	30
J. Fanshawe	15	73	21
E. Dunlop	14	64	22
M. Bell	13	91	14

Perth

M. Hammond	29	158	18
Mrs M. Reveley	27	95	28
J. Goldie	22	95	23
P. Hobbs	18	38	47
P. Monteith	17	97	18

Plumpton

M. Pipe	53	122	43
R. Rowe	18	130	14
T. P. McGovern	17	85	20
J. Jenkins	15	95	16
J. Neville	14	37	38

Pontefract

M. Johnston	14	121	12
D. Nicholls	14	125	11
J. L. Eyre	13	175	7
J. Dunlop	12	47	26
B. Hills	12	66	18

Redcar

M. Johnston	27	141	19
J. Gosden	21	59	36
Mrs M. Reveley	20	226	9
J. L. Eyre	17	164	10
J. Dunlop	15	63	24

Ripon

M. Johnston	25	138	18
T. Easterby	23	219	11
J. Dunlop	16	58	28
B. Hills	13	67	19
H. Cecil	12	29	41

Salisbury

R. Hannon	42	356	12
J. Dunlop	29	131	22
R. Charlton	14	70	20
M. Channon	13	169	8
I. Balding	12	128	9

Sandown Park

Flat			
Sir Michael Stoute	32	134	24
R. Hannon	29	278	10
P. Cole	20	80	25
J. Gosden	19	103	18
J. Dunlop	19	127	15
jumps			
M. Pipe	23	107	22
J. Old	21	73	29
N. Henderson	21	144	15
P. Nicholls	19	70	27
J. Gifford	19	174	11

Sedgefield

Mrs M. Reveley	73	310	24
G. M. Moore	30	146	21
Howard Johnson	28	210	13
B. Ellison	20	168	12
Denys Smith	17	90	19

Southwell

Flat (all-weather)			
S. R. Bowring	50	441	11
R. Hollinshead	48	481	10
M. Johnston	47	219	21
D. Nicholls	44	326	13
Mrs N. Macauley	44	461	10
jumps			
J. O'Shea	14	57	25
Mrs S. Smith	11	88	13
M. Pipe	10	50	20
J. Jenkins	9	59	15
P. Nicholls	9	18	50

Stratford-on-Avon

M. Pipe	42	167	25
P. Hobbs	20	102	20
N. Twiston-Davies	13	81	16
N. Henderson	12	46	26
Miss V. Williams	11	31	36

Taunton

M. Pipe	75	327	23
P. Hobbs	37	171	22
R. Hodges	25	214	12
P. Nicholls	22	137	16
K.Bishop	12	69	17

Thirsk

J. L. Eyre	19	177	11
D. Nicholls	18	209	9
M. Johnston	15	89	17
T. Easterby	15	210	7
T. D. Barron	14	129	11

Towcester

K.Bailey	17	81	21
Miss V. Williams	14	57	25
M. Pipe	14	55	26
Mrs S. Smith	13	92	14
N. Henderson	12	59	20

Uttoxeter

M. Pipe	43	188	23
N. Twiston-Davies	33	173	19
S. Brookshaw	29	177	16
P. Hobbs	24	120	20
J. J. O'Neill	20	83	24

Warwick

Flat			
B. Hills	15	57	26
J. Fanshawe	12	43	28
M. Pipe	11	33	33
R. Hannon	10	92	11
P. Cole	9	54	17
jumps			
M. Pipe	35	137	26
P. Hobbs	15	74	20
N. Twiston-Davies	15	101	15
O. Sherwood	12	46	26
Miss H. Knight	10	71	14

Wetherby

Mrs M. Reveley	62	248	25
T. Easterby	37	207	18
Mrs S. Smith	31	163	19
M. W. Easterby	21	162	13
P. Beaumont	14	93	15

Wincanton

P. Nicholls	55	199	28
M. Pipe	52	216	24
P. Hobbs	26	151	17
R. Alner	26	190	14
R. Hodges	13	167	8

Windsor

R. Hannon	44	323	14
B. Meehan	19	173	11
Sir Michael Stoute	18	62	29
J. Gosden	17	83	20
I. Balding	16	106	15

Wolverhampton

Flat (all-weather)			
N. Littmoden	84	606	14
R. Hollinshead	67	638	11
Sir Mark Prescott	50	156	32
M. Johnston	42	254	17
P. D. Evans	40	511	8
jumps			
M. Pipe	9	15	60
T. George	2	4	50
J. Jenkins	2	5	40
R. O'Sullivan	2	2	100
Ian Williams	1	3	33

Worcester

M. Pipe	69	234	30
K. Bailey	29	107	27
P. Bowen	27	149	18
P. Hobbs	27	159	17
P. Nicholls	23	84	27

Yarmouth

H. Cecil	29	86	34
C. Dwyer	18	155	12
C. Brittain	18	175	10
E. Dunlop	17	84	20
M. Bell	17	108	16

York

Sir Michael Stoute	26	139	19
P. Cole	20	132	15
H. Cecil	19	94	20
M. Johnston	19	174	11
T. Easterby	17	195	9

Betting Record

If you are inclined to heed John McCririck's advice on pages 67–8 and keep a record of your betting, here's where to enter it.

date	*stake*	*type of bet*	*selection*

odds	*type of race*	*result*	*running balance*

date	*stake*	*type of bet*	*selection*

odds	*type of race*	*result*	*running balance*

date	*stake*	*type of bet*	*selection*

odds	*type of race*	*result*	*running balance*

Index